SO-EKL-589

First Writes

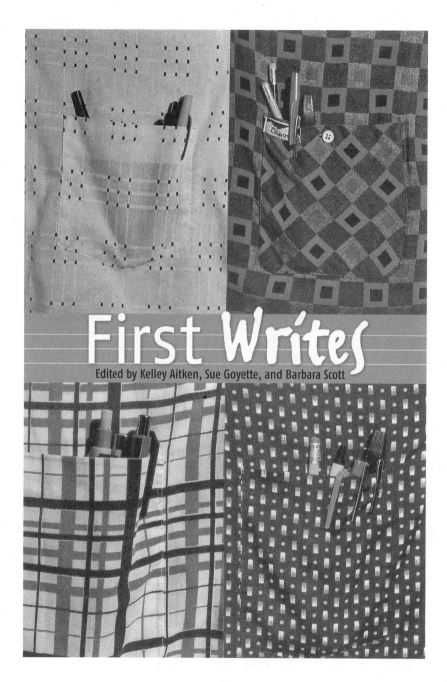

First Writes

Edited by Kelley Aitken, Sue Goyette, and Barbara Scott

THE BANFF CENTRE

PRESS

Copyright © 2005 Banff Centre Press. Individual authors retain copyright to their own work. All rights reserved. No part of this book may be reproduced, stored in a retrieval system or transmitted in any form or by any means without prior written permission from the publisher, or, in the case of photocopying or other reprographic copying, a licence from Access Copyright (The Canadian Copyright Licensing Agency), 1 Yonge Street, Suite 1900, Toronto, Ontario, Canada M5E 1E5 (www.accesscopyright.ca).

LIBRARY AND ARCHIVES CANADA CATALOGUING IN PUBLICATION

First writes / [edited by] Kelley Aitken, Sue Goyette and Barb Scott.
ISBN 1-894773-16-0

1. Authors and publishers—Canada.
2. Canadian literature—Publishing.
3. Canadian literature—20th century—History and criticism.
I. Aitken, Kelley, 1954– II. Goyette, Sue III. Scott, Barbara, 1957–

PS8081.1.F57 2005   C810.9'0054
C2005-900434-7

Copyedited by Kirsten Craven and
  Jennifer Nault
Book and cover design by Alan Brownoff
Cover photos by Paul Smith
Proofreading by Lesley Cameron
Printed and bound in Canada by Houghton
  Boston Printers, Saskatoon, Saskatchewan

Canada Council   Conseil des Arts
for the Arts   du Canada

Alberta Foundation for the Arts

The Banff Centre Press gratefully acknowledges the support of the Canada Council for the Arts and the Alberta Foundation for the Arts for its support of our publishing program.

THE BANFF CENTRE
PRESS

THE BANFF CENTRE PRESS
Box 1020
Banff, Alberta T1L 1H5
www.banffcentre.ca/press

Contents

KELLEY AITKEN

SUE GOYETTE

BARBARA SCOTT

Introduction

IN RECENT YEARS, much has been published about the writing process. But in that literature, there's a gap. What of the difficult transition from private to public, when that first manuscript becomes a book? How writers cope with first-time publication is as varied as the individuals themselves, yet when we opened the topic to the thirty-one writers represented here, we found quite a bit of common ground. Ask any writer to name the best moment in the entire experience of bringing out a book, and most will choose the one when they first found out they were to be published. It is like a moment out of a fantasy or fairy tale, when it seems your most extravagant wish has been granted. It is also a moment of utter innocence, before any of the realities of publishing and public space begin to intrude in the form of bad reviews, or no reviews, readings attended only by the publicist and bookstore owner, strained relationships with your publisher, or editor, even your colleagues.

That these aspects of the publishing experience exist is not news, but what may perhaps be surprising is how solitary this very public space can be. Our purpose in putting together this anthology was to enable a kind of conversation, a way for writers who've "been there" to talk across the silence to those who haven't been but hope to be, and who could use some helpful advice. In the process we discovered that the essays also have the character of war stories, with the power to remind us of what we've been through and what it took to get to the other side. Whether the writers of these essays writhe over the miasma of envy they once breathed about who was being nominated, reviewed, and praised, and/or vilified and ignored; or recount the enormous upheaval of family and culture that happened when they crossed into public space; or invite us to howl with them over the agent/publisher/colleague from hell; they offer a rich exchange, a way to bridge the gap between the solitudes all writers necessarily inhabit. In their honesty and generosity they remind us that, though we work in isolation, we are not alone. It's fitting that The Banff Centre Press is the publisher that has taken this project on, since the centre is where many of us took our first steps toward publication, and first took solace in and courage from being part of a tribe. We hope this anthology will have a similar effect.

So, from the tribe . . .

KELLEY AITKEN

Shame, or, Like Pain, the Memory of it Fades ...

SHAME.

Because I had no idea what it would be like to send my stories out there. Because the minute the book was published I knew it was flawed. Shame because I wasn't sure I'd captured it, that distilled interior country and my extraordinary communion with it and the things I learned about acceptance and human nature when I was slicing away, faceting those tiny bright jewels, as much mined as made, and of course the fact that I made them at all was sort of shocking, even to me. As extraordinary as the process was, as mirror and foil, friend and foe, now I had only the product to show for all that and, well, did I think someone would care?

The shame I felt after publication had to do with a certain sort of cluelessness. I'd fantasized about what it would be like to "be published," while ignoring certain facts about books: people read them; people judge them; and, depending on the book, people ignore them. I'd gone public with something hitherto hidden, not just what the stories were about, but the "how" of them. This is how I think! And see the world! And describe things!

Writing has been, in part, a battle with my own human nature. I think shame was part of my inspiration to write and still is. It's not the only one, of course, but it is in there, certainly, along with the bookworm's reverence for books; the delight in the variousness and accuracy of words; the yearning to express myself; and the need to structure an intense response to the sensate world. It may just be that shame is a part of my psychological makeup, and that writing concentrates that feeling into something workable, something I can wrestle to the ground and then step over.

Years ago in Calgary, I attended a Halloween party decked out as a jar of grape jelly. (I had a thing about containers, a lot of women do.) Already, in my illustrious — illustrative? — costume career, I had been a bottle of Heinz Ketchup, a tube of Crest, and a bottle of lithographer's ink or Tusche — there's a private printmaker's joke in there, but never mind. The jelly outfit consisted of purple tights, a purple turtleneck, and purple shoes, and, attached to my chest with safety pins, a piece of painted canvas cut in the trademark Welch's wedge. I'd gone the manufacturer's one further with my headgear: a Bacchanalian rig of felt leaves and pipe-cleaner vines.

At the party, I danced and joked, and mingled and drank the requisite number of beers, and then stayed the night with friends in the ground floor flat of the house where the party was held. The next morning, what with the to-ing and fro-ing between upstairs and down for coffee and a communal greasy breakfast (the ideal hangover cure), everyone remarked on a pair of lilac pantyhose — part of some girl's fairy costume, as I recall — which were strewn across the lawn. One can assume there had been an appropriate or, more accurately, inappropriate libation, and perhaps an invitation to dance from a local randy Oberon. It was clear from the telltale crotch smudge that the mauve fairy hadn't bothered with panties. I wanted to put a lot of distance between myself and those post-debauch gaunch. My purple tights — think royal, think opaque — were distinct from the discarded hose, which were sheer and pale. Yet, however much I protested that they weren't mine, I was mercilessly teased by the upstairs equivalent of the good-time gang, four or five easterners come to Calgary to make the big construction bucks. Well, everyone knows men are colour-blind.

Another woman might have laughed along with her tormentors instead of blushing and getting defensive. Another woman might have rolled Oberon for his knickers. Alas, another woman might not have gone to the party as a jar of jelly.

How often is that first book a kind of coming out, a leap from whatever closet or pantry or warehouse of heretofore unaired opinions. For years my honesty was under wraps. Steeped and kept in jars. My shit to myself. But, oh, the exhilaration of scribbling on a page, the furtive high, following that disloyal thought, that acid observation. I decided I was serious about writing and yearned, as most young or new writers do, for publication, not recognizing that the holy tussle and days of delirium, the hard truths and determined honesties of solitude might one day result in other people actually reading what I wrote.

When my book came out, so, in a sense, did I.

"Oh, it's fiction, is it?" Said with a knowing look. Your book is out there, but you're at home behind a locked door screaming yourself, well, purple at the assumption of autobiography.

And shame because, of course, it is.

We don't talk about this enough. We hedge and get coy and talk about "the story" and "the character" and "the image," using the removed and marvellously ambiguous language of literature to sidestep the question. We look down at the people who want to know. We arch our literary eyebrows at all this fascination with personality, this perverse insistence on the source of the stuff. We act as if in writing and publishing and reading to minuscule groups at a Chapters branch in Zihuatanejo, we're simply above the concerns of the *People*-reading herd. But the novice writer feels herself quail. Even as she bluffs her way past the inquisitiveness of friends and acquaintances, and that fledgling group — her reading public; even as she shilly-shallies and euphemizes, or just plain changes the subject, a part of her feels shame because to be a true writer, the Real Gen, she should have pulled that story out of thin air. There is supposed to be a vast gap between fiction and, God forbid, therapeutic writing, and in her heart of hearts, her *corazón de corazones*, she knows she wrote out of memory and perhaps even a desire to set one or many records straight. She can't absolutely guarantee there wasn't a kind of emotional/personal motivation behind it all and doesn't that make her just another sap with a pen and a journal? And so, maybe she doesn't have the get-up-and-go, or grit, or chutzpah, or fortitude, or real raw talent to be a writer.

Oh fuck off. I mean, that's where you have to end up. Give shame the boot, the old heave-ho. But you can't do that until you get under it, until you shovel it out of your own barn, or compost bin, and to do that, I think, you have to make your peace, okay, begin to make peace with two things: the claims of your own needy ego, and the relative insignificance of same.

We are all living stories, verb and participle, that is to say, each life is a story, a long and often deviating narrative, and those narratives breathe, they pump out oxygen. Our lives are our first inspiration; through them we participate in the larger culture and community, which uses story as its glue. The first sounds and shapes of language are those that define the contours of the world we are born and grow into, the small inside the large, and in the connection of the personal to the universal, the structure of story makes itself evident. Too la-de-da? Then look at it the other way around. It is the reverse process, writing so deeply into the memory of an experience that you actually see it for the first time and at that precise moment discover its essence as "story," a moment at which, no matter how many details match, it ceases to be autobiography. Because as a writer, you've seen the need to get out of the way. This is not, by the way, the same as the writerly habit of answering the dreaded "did that happen to you?" with the literary equivalent of "none of yer feckin' business."

What, after all, is so wrong with the question? Why do we never say, by way of response, "Well, yes and more; I went for a walk in my own life and fell through into story?" Why do we not answer honestly and openly what is simply a question from that same hunger in our reader for the meaning and connection that drives us to write?

Shame. Somebody somewhere defined good writing as impersonal, transcendent, stemming from pure imagination. Is there a test? Like one of those litmus papers that you hold against the typed page and if it turns blue it's a boy? Don't get me started on the whole gender thang, male versus female writing, emotional versus intellectual, psychological versus polit- ical, large versus small/domestic/intimate/personal, yadda, yadda.

Shame.

In an effort to get rid of it, I had to get under it. I had to come to grips with this prickly issue of autobiography. Was it my subject matter? Perhaps there's a more precise term out there. But I think, for many writers, fiction- from-life is less a confessional process than a kind of subconscious generosity. We donate moments from our past to the process, whose goal is a discrete entity within a continually evolving tradition. Because in writing, that isolated act, we move through to the collective, from the personal to our shared humanity.

The day after I launched the book in Ottawa, I had tea with an old friend at her sister's home. Commenting on one of my stories, my friend turned to her sister and said, "Word for word, that's exactly how it happened." With a single remark she had wiped out my work of months. Had I done nothing more than pin a snapshot to a page? But on the heels of my deflation came another thought: she's as convinced as if it happened that way. I had taken what occurred and wrestled with it and stared it in the face and cringed when it stared back, and then taken what none of us could possibly have known at the time and wedded it back into the living of it and thus made it a story. Because I had been as hard on myself as narrator/character as on all the other characters, she believed it to be true. In revealing the emotional truths of story, I had also created, for her, a new memory of the event.

Look, I know it's a solitary business, this writing stuff: hours of isolation, 1 per cent inspiration and 99 per cent perspiration, etc. But writing is essentially a tool of communication, there's creation and then there's reception, with publication as the dividing line. Once your work passes beyond that, it's out of your control. Lo and bloody behold, the reading of your work proves not to be a passive thing. Terrifying? Yes. But less obviously, sending your work out into the world is a liberating process. It's an act of engagement. Somehow, what I'd struggled over, shaped, and finally polished, managed to touch a few people. Against the insidious blooming of shame at having "gone public" were those few folks whose comments came back to me. That the book had moved them, captured something, distilled an experience of theirs, that they'd liked it. I had a small but worthy readership.

It mattered. The shitty thing about shame is that it can make you stop, or flounder, or try to please in that panicky way. It's the wrong tool to have in your kit bag when you're trying to do what's even harder than writing your first book, which is writing your second. Oh sure, the energy to write again would have to come from me. But when people responded to my work, they were giving me a leg up, they were helping in a way they might never understand.

The one sure thing about the publication of any book is that, eventually, it's in the past. The event and all the subsequent emotional fallout become pieces of your autobiography. Some years ago, at a dinner for just-back-from-Banff writers, a certain level-headed gal, in response to a pretentious comment made by a big-name author further down the table, uttered this *sotto voce* aside, "It's just a book."

I'm taking her remark as my writing motto. As a reader, there have been times in my life when books have pretty much saved me. There have been books that have changed the world. I cannot imagine an existence without them. And yet, whenever my ego goes into some new emotional paroxysm and yammers on about how hard writing is, and how no one understands, and how isolated it feels, and how embarrassing; or whenever the nakedness of the thing I've written threatens to undo me, I've learned to placate those twin gods of shame and inspiration. I've learned to turn my computer off. When the turquoise square collapses to black and my own reflection stares back at me, I wink and whisper: It's just a book.

PAUL ANDERSON

Survival
at Sea

IT SEEMS you may be spending some time at sea. If you are reading the contents of this bottle, you have plucked from the waves a set of sailing instructions I once wrote for myself, when publication of the book I was writing lay far beyond the horizon.

Before Setting Out
- Remember who matters.
- Remember what doesn't.
- Think of why you did this.
- Think of what could happen.
- Eat your greens and take your vitamins.

Choose an Epigraph
One that, in a pinch, might double as an epitaph. (Keep handy for burial at sea.)

I do not mind at all if the loud-mouthed, or flatterers, or the mock-modest, or fault-finders, gossips, tittle-tattlers, talebearers, or any sort of grumbler never see this book. I have never meant to write for them. So they can keep out of it. And so can all those learned men (and unlearned too) who are merely curious ...
—From *The Cloud of Unknowing*, Fourteenth Century, Anonymous

Put Your Affairs in Order

The ocean is big, and will not be controlled. Consider that:

- Some goals are good to pursue; others are good to reach.
- You cannot control the destination, nor can you know it before it appears, but you can still try, at least a little, to steer.
- Your task each morning is to begin thinking about the chapter you are working on.
- It is time to establish a liveable definition of success.

So, stop:

- Making time your enemy and tormentor.
- Dramatizing your plight.
- Interviewing yourself: plenty of time to brood afterwards — the time for regrets is when it's too late.
- Explaining and enumerating the many reasons why you have quit writing.

Plan for Shipwreck

Glance along the route you have charted, this time with an eye to shoals and reefs, and bad-weather havens to run for. These are the shores you and the wreckage will likely wash up on. In case of shipwreck, with no books to read, name the one you would write, to keep from losing your mind. To give it a place to live — food, water, and exercise. What kind of book would this be, what kind of place would it need? (They're all islands, finally.)

Let us take, for the sake of example, a novel. Well, a novel in the sense that the novel is that most fluid of imaginary forms, potentially as various as human experience itself. But though it contains many fictions, and so cannot be considered factually true, neither does it ask to be considered art.

Better, perhaps, to approach such a book as a small necropolis sprung up about an island tomb. Of an emperor, for instance, and his bride. Together, the temple complex, burial vault, and catafalque enshrine, about the corrupt and necrotic remnants of the tyrant, expressions of that civilization's high arts: frescoes, urns, weavings, jewellery, musical instruments, sculpture, architecture, myth...

But there is more to a city than the glorification of emperors, and so his necropolis houses not just art but latrines, barracks, brothels, stables, granaries, archives, palaces, altars, forges, cells, schools, market stalls. Imagine, now, that city sacked, despoiled, pilfered, shattered. If these are losses to historical science and beauty and permanence, not all is lost. For we begin to see that the sack of his city, the ruin of his empire, the desecration and the pilferage of his tomb and his bride's say things the emperor's artists could not. More even than the city intact, its ruins are a work of the imagination ...

Sand sifted into windowless rooms, arcades blasted by sand and wind down to goblet stems. Overhead, vaults of roosting doves; swatches of plaster not yet fallen; bolts of sun-weft motes unrolled from the wrack of a roof rift; rents of cloud in banquet halls; rainwater pooled on shards of tile. On the walls, down the halls, tapestries rotted to showy cobwebs; solemn sentries with chiselled-off noses and toes and phalluses; masks with jewelled eyes gouged blind; lovers' pledges scratched into frescoes.

Down the last passage lies a jimmied sarcophagus. Within this, the ashes of the absolute book are all that remain, its pages burned at the emperor's death, to give form to the defeat of form, to give Chaos her due.

Log Your Last Coordinates

- You have reached the point of no return — the book will not be fundamentally other than it is now.
- You have created great moments — long, fine stretches. Language and ideas, spirit and outrage, character and vision, wonder and imagination. Blood, bile, and sinew. Even bits of craft. But even after all you have given, the pages do not self-combust.

Home from the Sea

Survival at sea looks different from here. And the most precious thing I take from these instructions is that I wanted to preserve them, for someone. Two years have passed and the book has hit the shelves, but I recognize the creature who wrote these lines and feel a solidarity with his (and possibly your) plight. The book I was writing then was the rawest extension of a nervous system open to the elements. You could have scratched a sentence on Alpha Centauri and watched its author writhe in Calgary. Now it is no longer a part of me, already beginning to go its own way.

And it is with a reduced sense of urgency that I return to consider the many reasons why I have quit writing.

 Faking It

I CAN'T BE SURE (not having read the rest of this collection), but I would guess that I am uniquely unqualified to be in this anthology. Why? Because I don't have a book published. Well, I do and I don't. I've self-published with a group.

There are many stereotypes attached to the term "self-publisher." And there's a big difference between "self" and "vanity" publishers. Vanity publishers are independent companies who often pose as commercial publishers. They "accept" your manuscript submission with heaps of flattery, but their sole source of income is you, the author. Self-publishers know in advance that they are publishing themselves. Like any do-it-yourself project, self-publishing produces a range of results, from the forgettable to the best-seller.

My first encounter with self-publishing (at an impressionable age) was as a typesetter for the "forgettable" variety and this experience coloured my opinion for years. I thought of self-publishers as the writers no one else would publish. The windbaggy old man, miffed at his handful of polite rejection letters, who says, "I'll show 'em!" The pioneering sort who shakes a defiant fist and plunges into new territory. I never would have ventured into self-publishing if I hadn't fallen into it. More importantly, I did not do it alone but in a group, the Seven Sisters Writing Group. We started meeting in 1997. Our roll call has changed over the years, but the publishers are Billie Livingston, Shamina Senaratne, Sara Graefe, Judy MacInnes Jr., Andrea

Galbraith, Susan MacRae, Molly (Starlight) Morin, Shannon Cooley, Natalie Meisner, Lia Talia, and me. Yes, there are more than seven of us.

In 1998, someone had the bright idea to submit a proposal to the Vancouver International Writer's Festival. After a few years of bumming around the writing and publishing scene, we had developed a sense of who was reading and how we might rate in comparison. Luckily, the festival often reserves a couple of spots for emerging writers and we thought we had a chance of fitting that bill. We were not complete unknowns, some had previous publishing credits or book deals twinkling in the future. We were a loose, informal bunch, but the act of submitting a proposal forced us to coalesce and come up with a group name. Lo and behold, the festival accepted us. So then we needed a book to sell. That's the whole point of festivals. We pooled our money to print our first anthology: *Seven Sisters*. Even though we had the advantage of some editing, design, and marketing skills among our members, it was a lot of work. The book *and* the reading.

The work was worth it though. Despite the negative stereotypes, many of us in the group feel that self-publishing has inherent value. Susan says, "All readers and writers need to be challenged, and self-publishing is one way to get the work out there, and basically, to create a more diverse market for the reading public." Andrea sees self-publishing as a way to maintain creative self-control "to produce a book the way we want to."

For us, working as a group put a different spin on self-publishing. The book is "a project of the collective," which has a less self-serving ring to it. Andrea says, "I think people see it [the anthology] as a special and unique project, not somebody paying to print a book because no one else will."

Once the anthology was released and the festival program distributed, we were surprised to discover that the group was an entity. People started saying they'd heard of us before. We sent out proposals and booked readings at Word on the Street and the Vancouver library. At one reading, we looked around the crowded room with suspicion, wondering who all the people were. *Are they your friends? No, yours? Family?* We designed our own Web site, stumbled into a few print and radio interviews. In 2000, we published our second anthology, *Lady Driven*, and read at the Writer's Festival again in 2002.

These efforts have resulted in a group persona that is separate from our individual selves. This makes promoting the anthology, or a reading, less terrifying because it is less personal. We treat the promotion of the anthology (and the group) as if we are professionals working for a publishing company.

Publishing as a group can teach you, in a relatively safe environment, basic concepts of promotion. For Shamina, our anthologies are "elaborate calling cards." We have certainly used them this way. A book is tangible proof that we are committed to our writing and have an understanding of the publisher's point of view. Billie feels that working on communal projects puts you more in the mindset of how best to promote yourself.

We have been lucky. The readings, interviews, and anthologies have coincided so that no one event has happened in a vacuum. That's one of the promotion concepts we've learned. Publishing a book (or organizing a reading) in a void is fatal.

I still wouldn't say that self-publishing is inherently better than conventional publishing. Our experience has been fun and we have had the thrill of seeing our names pop up now and then, but it has also been a lot of work. It took money out of our pockets. There are never guarantees. As well, the work of self-publishing can quickly take over your life. There will always be someone to phone, a reading to organize, a poster to design. Eventually, you find yourself promoting a body of work that has become a hollow shell, an old and dried-out husk. In addition, doing it on your own can mean you miss out on valuable critique from an impartial and informed editor. However, I feel that self-publishing has its place within the larger picture of writing and publishing.

For one thing, there is a lot of pressure on writers, especially those of us who are still "emerging," to be market savvy. Every time you turn around, someone is offering a workshop on pitching to agents or marketing techniques. It does seem, some days, that the effort of good writing is no longer good enough. We also have to be shaking hands, forging connections, selling our ideas, targeting potential markets.

One thing that my experience with the two anthologies has taught me is that the writing mind and the publishing mind are two very different beasts that should be kept in their separate cages until their time to appear arrives. This may apply to conventionally published authors as well, because the book touring experience (from what I have observed) throws you into "marketing mode."

The writing mind does the initial work. Thinking about the market is the worst thing you can do when you are composing your poem or piece of prose. The market is fickle and the landscape will change by the time your piece is finished. For me, the actual process of writing requires hours in a room all by myself. If I'm not being true to my own material and voice, I have no reason to write. Because, as I well know, I'm not doing this for the money.

Once the piece is done, the writing mind needs to retreat into the background and let the publishing mind have its day. The writing mind doesn't understand that your work probably appeals to a small market, that consumers need some convincing to spend money on a book, that the printing cost will take up the lion's share of the list price, that maybe the first readings will be gratis, or that sales will be slow.

The process of self-publishing and self-promoting has perhaps made our group more calculating in ways, but we have also become more realistic about the publishing industry and ourselves as writers. We have a better idea of how much effort and money goes into a book, not just the production, but the marketing and selling of the darned thing. The experience gave us the feeling that we were taking an active part in our careers, pushing ourselves forward. It's important for struggling writers to feel they have some power over their fate. Susan hopes that our experience will give "hope to other writers starting out that this is another way to get their work out there — through collaborative effort. That's a good message to send out to writers."

I also remind myself that throughout history, the distinction between author and publisher is often pretty blurry. Many have worked on both sides of the desk. Dickens, for instance, published the initial serialized versions of *A Tale of Two Cities* and *Great Expectations* in his own magazine. More recently, Dave Eggers has built a reputation on publishing himself and his friends. Many well-known Canadian authors, such as Al Purdy and bill bissett, have pushed their careers forward by publishing themselves. And it's even possible to make money at it: Joe Garner and David Perrin are two self-publishers who have produced B.C. best-sellers.

Through collaborating on the two anthologies, we discovered a surprising source of potential and ability. Our next goal is to convince a company to publish our third anthology, leaving us to concentrate on the writing. But then again, we might do something different. Anything is possible. In the meantime, speaking for the collective, I hope you will recognize us someday soon in a bookstore near you.

Xcellent

ſew ít waſ erlee 60ſ n i was nevr getting publishd aneewher it seemd interminabul terribul not 4 aneething othr thn 2 partisipate in th world my independent politikul vizual n sound poet frends as well we wer all nevr getting publishd sew i startid blewointment-press th rejecksyun slips wer getting 2 weird like being shut out sew i publishd myself n poets who wer similarlee n diffrentlee leeding n being othr serches thn thos who wer getting publishd i publishd myself lance farrell bpNichol martina clinton judith copithorne maxine gadd sam perry david melville michael coutts david cull beth jankola d.a.levy uv kours manee othrs thn n as time went on if iuv 4gottn sum uv th erlee wuns thats inevitabul i spose thees tho wer th bases around me we talkd abt poetree wanting 2 xploor vizual sound non narrativ bridges n being btween th reedr n th work opning 2gethr in manee wayze

its 1965 still publishing myself in th blewointmentpress magazeen format using all kinds uv media n papr n papr insert approaches n veree inklusyunaree editorial approach as well not reelee going 4 anee wun or evn a few schools or approaches xciting bcoz evenshulee bwp publishd almost evreewun n from manee places yewnitid states england europe south amrika at ths time erlee mid sixteez me n barrie nichol wer sew oftn writing each othr talking abt th pome how much mor opend it cud b n opning sew much blewoint mentpress was starting 2 publish bpNichol in its pages thn barrie nichol wantid 2 dew a whol book uv my writing amayzing sew wundrful it wud b calld *we sleep inside each othr all* from his ganglia press me in van barrie in toronto parshulee in my eagrness it seemd 2 me 2 take a veree long time 2 publish i grew impatient in a veree benign way as ths was 2 b my veree first book evr awesum sew with blewointment n veree stone hous i was partrs with seymour mayne jim brown n patrick lane in veree stone hous we plannd 2 begin by publishing each uv ourselvs n thn publish onlee othrs wch did wundrfulee happn my book a blewoint-ment-veree stone hous co-produksyun was calld *fires in th tempul OR th jinx ship n othr trips* sew heers me in th west hand printing a lot uv it whil barrie in toronto is getting *we sleep inside each othr all* dun th 2 books may have bin neck n neck it was 1965–66 barrie was dewing a reeding at ubc he drove out 2 van n had boxes uv my book in his trunk 4 me xcellent veree beautiful covr stock glue bound covr drawing iud dun in a beautiful shade uv green reelee well printid n beautifulee presentid reelee my first book tho *fires in th tempul* was sew neck n neck as i sd i think no wun agrees on wch is my first book

fires in th tempul OR th jinx ship n othr trips covr uv an xcellent nude woman reeding n th inside mostlee offset printing with a mimeographd n quite thik stapuld in seksyun with nu chants fires in th tempul speeking n othrs in it wch i had printid myself with th mimeograph masheen xcellent sew xciting 1965–66 2 books releessd at th same time or diffrentlee timed dpending on wch provins n citee yu wud b in toronto vancouvr uv kours th time it tuk 2 drive *we sleep inside each othr all* 2 van was by wch time reelee *fires in th tempul OR th jinx ship n othr trips* had alredee bin releesd it was sew neck in neck in a great way

Travels without a Map

THE NIGHT I RECEIVED the mock-up cover of my novel, *Talon*, we had a hurricane in Jasper. Well, all right, it isn't really possible to have a hurricane in the middle of the Rocky Mountains, but it was trying like hell to be one. The winds were ferocious and the rain could have ripped the skin off dogs.

All that day, my publisher had tried to send me a PDF file, but my poor computer just didn't have the jam to receive it. I called the local library and asked the wonderful people there if they would mind receiving said file and printing the bugger up for me. They said for a five dollar fee, they would. My neighbour Connie, who works there as a librarian, said she could drop it off on her way home. The hurricane increased its fury ...

Was the cover going to be as beautiful as I thought it could be? Or was it going to be too difficult to reproduce the photograph? When Connie finally got to my house, I was afraid. I felt as though she was catching me naked; this was the first time anyone had seen my idea for the cover of my first novel. She handed me a plain cardboard folder. I opened it slowly and started crying when I saw the image. It was the most beautiful thing I had ever laid eyes on — besides my husband the day we were married and my son the day he was born. By the time she left my porch, that crusty old librarian was crying too.

That's what it feels like to publish a book.

As I wrote this sentence, I heard a thump. A sparrow had hit the front porch window. He was flying really fast, saw the reflection of the darkening night sky and, thinking he was safe, flew even faster. Then he hit the glass.

That too is what it feels like to publish a book.

You fly blind, travel without a map. The only signposts you have are your unfounded belief in the work itself, and the kindness of strangers who will sometimes lift you from the porch floor.

October 12, 2000
Dear Paulette,

Please accept this letter as an indication of NeWest Press's interest in developing and eventually publishing your manuscript, Talon. *I am pleased to tell you that at a recent board meeting our board was very enthusiastic about the possibilities of your manuscript. As you already know, Thomas Wharton will be working with you to adjust the narrative structure ...*

I'm going to publish a novel! I'll buy those Hungry Man dinners André loves so much for us to celebrate tonight. I'll quit my teaching job and write full time.

Wait a second.

What do they mean by "developing" and "adjusting the narrative structure"? I gave them a manuscript of poetry for pity's sake — what narrative structure? They want a novel? I don't know how to write a novel. I write poetry! How do I turn a two hundred–page manuscript of poetry into a novel?

Forty-three e-mails, nine months, and three rewrites later ...

July 13, 2001
Dear Paulette,

It is with the greatest of pleasure I write to inform you that NeWest has accepted your manuscript for publication in the Spring 2002 season ...

Once I signed the contract and filled out the obligatory "Author Statement" pages, I was a different person. I looked different, I was pretty sure. You know how after you have sex for the first time you're sure everyone can tell. Same thing here. There is a glow, there is a smell … there is a smile that not even teaching junior high can erase.

"Hey, Madame! I have a hamster. In my pants! Wanna see?"
"No, thank you, Troy. Perhaps you would like to take the rest of the afternoon off to return said hamster to its domicile."
"What?"
"Leave."
"Wow, Madame, thanks!"

And I think, "Before you go, I could sign that hamster of yours, I'm a published author, you know."

Author Statement Information — Biography — details should include where you were born
Why? Who cares if I was born in small town Alberta?

and raised
If I had been raised by bees it might be interesting, why did my parents have to be so normal? I will never get on Oprah.

what your hobbies are
I read and hike … oh God! Boring alert! I will say instead that I skydive and am an amateur archeologist — cleaning out André's bedroom certainly qualifies me for that.

Interesting anecdotes about your personal or professional life
If I had any interesting anecdotes, I would write a fucking memoir, not fiction.

your family
Raymond is my husband, but is there a more politically correct term? How about partner, spouse, second half of a parental unit, life partner? Will we

be together for a lifetime? Or does it mean he is my partner for the day-to-day stuff? What about André? Is he my son, a digit, a byte, an offspring, my boy, my pride and joy, a treasure I'd like to bury sometimes?

your habits
Don't go there, if they knew I smoked there would be all sorts of turned-up noses and sniffing going on, and when we go to a restaurant and the waiter asks, "Smoking or non?" everyone will look at me and when I say nonsmoking, they will politely protest, but really who in their right mind smokes while they eat? That's just wrong. So I will say that I jog. No, screw that, need shoe and kilometre vocabulary ... I'll leave it blank.

And then, I hit the window ...

October 1, 2001
Hi Paulette,

It's me, a representative of the press, who has made the suggestion that publishing may have to be postponed.

I know it really sucks to hear this, doesn't it? I should have clarified why I was talking about next fall ...

Cheers from,
your friendly face of cold water

Pre-Press Information
No, I don't know any "recognized authorities on the book's subject who might be willing to read galleys and make comments." Hey! Wait a second! There are authorities on this subject. My matante Alice, and my mom and dad, and Raymond's mom, and anyone born into French-Canadian families in Alberta. But wait, if they read this, they will hate it. The people in *Talon* aren't always "nice," and that was one rule we all lived by — what others see, counts. So if the characters here don't always get along, that's for the family to know, not everyone and their dog. So, no. No experts, and no one I know can actually read this after all. Well, there go the sales!

And no, there are no other books "similar to mine in content, approach, and appeal." My work is unique and original. Grandiose? Precious? Trite? This is like hell.

Were there any unusual or amusing incidents connected with the book's writing?
My roof leaked on and off for the two years I wrote the damned thing, and then stopped when I finally "put the baby to bed." I developed abnormal cells in my cervix, had a course of radiation, and bled ash for a week. My preconceived notions of good and evil were blown wide open. I was never so scared, nor as happy as when as I was writing this book. I now know without a doubt that I am never, ever, alone.

I learned that there is a masochistic streak a mile long and two miles wide in every writer. It expands proportionally with every page you write and disproportionally with every rejection slip you receive. It is incredibly strong and has the twisted appeal only an addict can understand.

Other than that, nope, nothing unusual to report.

July 28, 2002, 8 P.M.
Hi Paulette,

Try the earlier version — I realize that what I have saved here and what you sent me are two different versions but maybe we can work "between" the two of them if you are ok with that. It means going over the galleys and your version at the same time to make certain all the edits are ok with you. Go over the galleys with a blue pencil maybe? That way I can tell the difference between your edits and the proofreader's edit marks.

Thanks for the lavender eye mask. My eyes do hurt after a while because I forget to blink! We have a deadline here so if you could get these back a.s.a.p. that would really be appreciated …

My mother-in-law insists that I go up to Lac La Biche for her birthday. I need to take a bus to Edmonton to hitch a ride with my sister-in-law, since

Raymond and André are already up there. That leaves me two days to do this. I can do this. I have to do this because we leave from Lac La Biche to go shrimp fishing for three weeks. My sister and her partner need help for this last year on their boat. They are both so crippled from the rigours of fishing that if we don't help them out, they will not fish this season.

So we go.

So it goes.

August 23, 2002, 5:44 P.M.
Hi again, Paulette,

So, again I am sorry it has taken so long, but I did get word from the publisher that you may use the section on Bloodstoppers as described in your e-mail on these conditions . . . you have acquired permissions for the songs, correct? It would be awkward if they could not be used. That would mean . . .

Never mind what that would mean! I know what that means, I can feel it. Another fucking window, and there's the cold, hard floor. Okay, I have to get permission from Barachois to use parts of the songs that they wrote. Is this going to cost me? I have no money. They will know I have no money, right? Next book, I write my own damned songs!

Hélène Arsenault, from the now-defunct Acadian group, Barachois, picks me up off the floor . . .

September 2, 2002, 8:56 A.M.
Hello Paulette,
Do you remember which band member you were talking to about the use of the song in your book? What you put in the credits seems fine. And yes, we would love to have a copy of the book!!

Yes, of course, that is what it boils down to: people will read my book. That's what publishing affords me. It's both thrilling and terrifying, like flying, like flying naked.

As far as writing goes, I still travel without a map. For that to work, I have to trust my work. And to that end, I will continue to fly, furtively scanning the horizon for hurricanes. I will continue to fly head-on, blindly, sometimes into the welcoming wide blue sky, sometimes into windows.

ERIC FOLSOM

The **Invention** of the Valley

MY FIRST BOOK wasn't meant to be my first book, in fact I didn't think it would appear as a book at all. During the year when the idea that turned into *Poems for Little Cataraqui* occurred to me, I was looking for money, as usual, applying for grants, and working on the nth version of an assortment of poems about my love life. Nobody seemed to have any great interest in my love life then, least of all the editors at the literary presses. In hindsight, I can hardly blame them, since not very much was actually happening and the poems themselves were far too personal and much too obscure.

In 1991, the Kingston Artists' Association, which recently morphed into the Modern Fuel Artist-Run Centre, received funding for a ten-year art event called the Millennium Project/Art for Earth's Sake. Each year, four or five artists would be paid to create an outdoor sculpture, environmental art, or some all-around happening — conceptually, things were pretty loose. The works were to be located in a conservation area north of Kingston, Ontario, the Little Cataraqui Conservation Area, named after a creek that flows through it. The theme would be the Reintegration of Man and Nature.

In 1993, I got word that the organizers of the project were interested in applications from outside the visual arts community, and I figured I suited the description. The grants were for one thousand dollars, and for that sum I proposed to write a series of poems in free verse covering the history of the Little Cataraqui watershed since the last ice age. About ten thousand years in twenty poems. I would read the poems aloud, on-site, on the opening day of the project. The words would be heard and then disappear, thus reintegrating themselves and perhaps us with Nature. The organizers liked the idea and approved the proposal three months before I had to give the reading.

I did some research at the local archives, located at Queen's University, and I contacted the very helpful Kingston Archaeological Centre, all in my spare time since I still had small children to care for, and was also writing book reviews for the local newspaper. At six weeks, I cut off the research and began to write madly — about four weeks of rough draft and two weeks for polishing. I tend to be verbose, given the chance, so the rushed effort was probably a good thing. I had no time to run off at the mouth.

On the opening day, people came and I read the poems in a loud voice, while we sat in the ruined foundation of an old barn under a fiercely hot July sun, three shows in one day. I got paid and the Kingston Artists' Association put articles about the Millennium Project in their newsletter, put videos in their archives, and I thought that was the end of the story. Back on the list of things to do went my poems about unrequited love. I hadn't counted on Joe Blades.

Joe and I hadn't actually met at this point, but we knew each other as publishers of small poetry magazines, the kind of homegrown litzines that nurture unknowns and generally get ignored by published writers. It's a good way to find your own cohort and invent your own audience. This was well before the Internet became a common feature on the landscape, so literary business was conducted through the mail, and editors usually traded copies of their zines with each other to keep up with the scene. Joe's magazine was *New Muse of Contempt*, and mine was *Next Exit*. Joe later told me he'd been hanging around in Fredericton's artist-run gallery one day, looking through the newsletters that such galleries send each other — more cross-pollination via the printed word. He noticed my name and a description of the Millennium Project, and he was kind enough to contact me and inquire about what I had done. Had the work been published?

Would I like to send the manuscript to Joe's book imprint, Broken Jaw Press? You bet I would.

Poems for Little Cataraqui, the book I hadn't thought was a book, and a book that shamelessly ignores the sorrows of love, was published by Broken Jaw in the fall of 1994. It was one of Joe's earliest titles and, as with upstart magazines and readings beside old barns, I had the sense we were creating our own audience, one reader at a time. We had hardly any reviews outside the zine community that already knew us, but it was a book! My name was on a stack of pressed wood pulp. I could officially call myself a poet and the League of Canadian Poets and the Canada Council would have to agree. Still, the majority of the people who noticed the book only did so because we waved it in their faces. I set up a reading tour across southern Ontario, slept on a lot of couches, and began to slip into the weird twilight world of the visiting artist. If you're from somewhere else you might be important. But at most venues, the locals are there to hear their friends read, and you had better politely acknowledge the genius of all the other poets and get used to the "isn't it swell to be geniuses together" kind of evening. Remember, one reader at a time.

If there's a moral to this tale, I'm not completely sure what it is. It might be: Try anything, you just never know. Or the moral I most need to bear in mind: Shut up and do your damn work. Just maybe, however, the moral is more complex. Even today, writing what I hope will be a fourth book, wondering who on earth will be interested in such obscure and wacko stuff, I'm aware that nothing has gotten any easier. The audience is still elusive and gained one person at a time. The infrastructure that supports Canadian literature is still held together with masking tape and a government grant, either of which could give way at any moment. The plain old public space, into which we as writers step, must be reinvented every time, especially if we claim to be creating art, not virtually identical commercial products.

This challenge never goes away or becomes less pressing. It could be the real point of writing: breaking down the relentless private world enveloping us, and making a truly public realm happen. Most commercial literature, though I honestly admire and even envy the artistry that creates it, is a service sold for money, and those in pursuit of money (or fame, or gravitas) quite naturally wish to influence the outcome. Their effort at control typically results in greater and greater restrictions on formerly open, inclusive forms of art. As we've seen with rock music, art forms can stagnate, artists can become increasingly professional, and audiences increasingly infantile. Book clubs, casual discussions, and fan Web sites can moderate the loss, providing the reader with a feeling of participation, but generally an author's work is projected onto the consuming public, like an image on a blank screen.

The commercial goal is to create demand, not to create discussion, and certainly not to create the legends, symbols, and cultural narratives that support the realm of public imagining. Where the actual retail sale is admittedly a public exchange between the writer and their audience, the eventual transaction of reading is private and almost never subsequently discussed. Thus we have the simulation of a public event, a false spectacle rather like the ones that rule our national political campaigns, where the objective is face-time in the media for politicians, not real encounters with real voters.

Of course, there's nothing wrong with consuming the latest mystery thriller privately, but what if the only time something truly creative and new happens is when we meet out in the open? Maybe the audience and the writers who belong to them form one continuum, one community that wants some aspect of its life acknowledged. When writers and audiences are really in touch, it's a way for everyone in the group to be seen and heard publicly, a chance to see and hear about our neighbours and our own neighbourhood. Think about art as a way of creating meaning for ourselves, and who are we after all? It's us in our small townships, our medium-sized cities, and our suburban sprawls, in all the places that haven't been written about. Maybe that's why a book about a tiny valley just over the hill from the 401 got published. Some even claim to like the poems.

As my parting piece of advice, if you're a writer, use the details of your romantic life sparingly — or not at all. Get out of the house and see what the other artists, writers, and musicians are doing. You could use some fresh air. Consider running a reading series, hosting workshops, starting a magazine, or publishing chapbooks. Remember, here at the grassroots, you are the infrastructure. Tell your neighbours and your relatives to come out to the old barn north of the highway, two o'clock next Sunday, for your poetry extravaganza. Tell them to bring some lawn chairs. Tell them you're doing this thing from the ground up.

Protection

I LIVE IN A SMALL ENOUGH TOWN, so small that the Purolator guy, who delivered the box of my books, was the same guy who had coached my son's baseball team that summer. He had threatened to check if they were wearing their cups with his baseball bat before every game. We assumed he was kidding, but still, it was with that thought that I reached out to take my books from him. You have to keep yourself protected, he had said that summer, thumping the bat against the side of his foot. Indeed.

I'd like to say that when my first book came out it was that easy, that I was a lot like my son when he was six and first had to wear a jock strap, that in some metaphorical way, I too had a sort of armour on and could walk into the corners of tables and chairs, thinking I had found some miraculous cure for vulnerability. "It doesn't even hurt," he'd say, banging into opened cupboards, doors. But I'd be lying. The way you feel when your book is published has more to do with the way you feel when you do anything in public than with the actual book itself. It's another Zenlike way to take a good look at how you move in the world.

Ideally, a book is an important way of enclosing an epoch of ideas, a meadow fenced off with sections, page numbers, and two covers that keep the poems or stories that are grazing on your blank pages together. In that sense, a book is a marking of your trail, the leaning spruce split by lightning you use as a kind of compass point in your artistic terrain. Important. And if

I was a centred, calm kind of Yoda-person, that would be that. I'd unmoor the book and leave it to float off into the world, concerned only with the paper in front of me, my small fire of new ideas and the long night to burn them.

Letting go of something is a challenge, especially when it was hatched from the heart and relayed by the hand. Some of us choose to eat vast amounts of peanut M&Ms, shake the Magic 8 ball until it gives the right answer, and some of us take every fortune from every fortune cookie as some celestial prediction for the lonely book making its way in the world. "You would make a good lawyer" momentarily stumped me, until I figured that someone would end up suing me over one of my poems and I, being unemployed, would have to be my own counsel. But we all have our own way of translating the world and I can't be the only one out here pushing the repeat button on the stereo, listening to the same song all night to perpetuate the feeling of doom that pervades me once in a while.

Sure I'd take my daughter to Chapters to see me shelved near Glück and Hirshfield, and sure I kind of believed Robyn when she said, "Maybe they sold out of yours," when my book wasn't there. And sure I drank my fair share of Kilkenny and danced my ass off with a lovely bunch of men from Waterford when the review in the *Globe* was good. I have few regrets, chalking it up to being a learning experience. "You don't have to say every-thing you're thinking, especially if there's a microphone in front of you," is one important lesson that should be in the first chapter of every getting published manual. Another, "Don't wear that new front closure bra to a reading without making sure the hook is, well, hooked." If I could wind the big clock backwards and go back to myself standing in the rain of the morning after the first reading I gave from the book, I'd tell myself two things: one: Don't let the bastards in. And two: For the love of God, no one needs two suitcases for a three-stop tour — all your clothes are black and how many shirts does one girl need?

By "bastards," I mean anyone or anything. And by "in," I mean past the drawbridge, through the big stone gates to that secret castle of self where the true writer lives and works. No one goes into the room where you take the straw of your days and spin gold. No one. No well-meaning inquisitive reader who wants your metaphor dictionary to figure out what you meant by that third bird for a paper they're doing, not the critic who has figured out what the third bird means and wants to tell you exactly what you're doing. Perhaps good reviews, and bad, can get close to your work, perch on its lines and peck the I's right out of it, talk about your strengths, your weaknesses until the cows come home, and maybe you'll hear something worthwhile, something that sounds your intuitive bell of truth. You take that bit of truth to improve your craft, you say thank you, but then you close the door and you get back to work.

It's hard enough facing the bottomless pit of the page, it's hard enough to sit and wait, rubbing the clouds and coffee of that day together until you get a spark of an idea that you'd follow anywhere. You've climbed the steep trail of sending it out there, having it returned, of wondering if it's worth it, or all a waste of time, and really, what else is there to say that hasn't been said brilliantly already? And yet, daily you alchemize the heartbreaks, the routine of "being domestic as a plate," you coax the shine out of the tarnished, tired days and with great patience and relentless attention, you find the hummingbird heart embedded in each piece and gently, oh so carefully, you coax it to beat on its own. Remember the feeling when it does, remember the pure joy of pushing up your sleeves, bending over it. Remember the intent. Because that's what is more important. The book is the product, a fine product, but the work is what gives you, in day-after-day doses, your purpose.

So I'm facing myself, I've whiplashed time and am back in Vancouver the morning after the first reading. I know I stood in my room at the Sylvia Hotel the night before and changed my shirt three times thinking, this black shirt or this black shirt or this black shirt? I know I called my sister collect in New York just to hear her voice tell me it was going to be okay. I know I sat on the bed and imagined the blank stares of incomprehension after each poem. I know I was scared. I know that I read with someone who told the audience that he'd stopped writing poetry in high school, that it was a teenager kind of thing to do. I know that "scared" is a polite word, a word that doesn't encompass the wilderness of terror that was on my trail. I know that somehow the book was already in past tense, that I'd stepped into the clearing on the other side of being published and it was a place I didn't know myself in yet, and that the slow process of collecting, of ordering and writing it down had already started. The last thing I'd tell my younger self would be to parody that Purolator/baseball coach with his well-intentioned threat. You better be wearing your cup. You gotta protect yourself out there. But I wouldn't carry the baseball bat. It's a metaphor after all. And writers are such vulnerable creatures, we want our lessons to be, oh, so gentle, simple even.

Arriving at a First Book

We Who Can Fly

MY FIRST BOOK WAS BORN of a sea of rejection slips.

I'd been a graduate student at the University of Toronto in the 1960s and had gathered a group that started a literary magazine, which published Margaret Atwood, Margaret Avison, Gary Geddes, Dennis Lee, and me, among others. Then I moved to Kingston to teach, and I spent years writing in isolation. I started writing groups. I worked on *Quarry*. Nothing got me past the wall. After twenty years, I was discouraged.

Then in the winter of 1991–92 two acceptances came within months, one from *Descant*, the other in an unprepossessing, almost unnoticeable envelope from the writing studios at Banff. I was so surprised, I could barely pick up the phone to say I was coming.

I learned later that every application to Banff goes through three tiers of readers, but I couldn't (and still don't) believe I would have been accepted if Adele Wiseman hadn't been the director of the writing program. Not many people can read beneath the surface of writing to the intention, but I'm sure she was one of them.

I'D HOPED ADELE would go over my work with me at Banff, but I learned just weeks before I was to go that she had stomach cancer. When I arrived, my editor, Rachel Wyatt, told me that Adele was too sick to sit on a plane.

Even without Adele's skill and support, the six weeks of the May studios changed my life. It didn't get me past the rejection slips, but it did introduce me to other writers; it was the beginning of a literary life, and it did lead to my first book.

Back home, my colleague Tom Marshall suggested that I might "do some work" on Adele. I had taught her novel *Crackpot* for years and I knew she had not attracted much critical discussion. In the fall of 1992, I submitted a proposal to ACCUTE (Association of Canadian College and University Teachers of English) to give a talk on Adele at their annual conference. To my astonishment, the proposal was accepted. I vowed that if the talk went well, I would do a book on Adele.

The talk was well received, and I returned to Kingston, faced with my vow to do the book, unsure where to start. Many of Adele's friends had spoken about her at her memorial service (she had died the year before on June 1, 1992). What they had said would make a fine basis for a book, but they all seemed to live in a charmed circle of creativity and freedom beyond my reach. I felt confined by the demands of my job, motherhood, the sidewalks of my daily life. Banff had given me some contacts, though. Rachel Wyatt had been a close friend of Adele's; Mary Lou Dickinson, who had been there with me, had long known Adele and her daughter, Tamara.

Gradually the book took shape as an anthology of reminiscences, poetry, and critical essays. Rachel gave me names and addresses of possible contributors; Tamara suggested others and agreed to write a piece herself. She also gave me permission to include Adele's last story, "Goon of the Moon and the Expendables," and to read her mother's papers in the York archives.

I have worked in archives before, but York's reading room is one of the most beautiful I've encountered, with its several portraits of Margaret Laurence and its painting of the river that runs both ways. The poet Hilda Doolittle said of her own writing, "I have gambled with eternity," and in the York archives, one is very aware that Margaret Laurence and Adele made bets with the future. And won.

The Adele Wiseman archive is enormous, over a hundred boxes, and it had not been completely catalogued by early 1995. I decided to start with the poetry. I knew Adele had published five or six poems, and that she had been working on a long poem, "The Dowager Empress," but I was astonished to discover three boxes of short poems dating from 1982 to 1987. I had met Adele in 1982, so this was what she was working on in the years I knew her and corresponded with her.

The poetry was mostly rhymed, which was not fashionable in 1995, less so in the 1980s when Adele was writing it. Not every poem was memorable, but as Tom Marshall had said, one of the strengths of Adele's work was her cumulative power, and this poetry had cumulative power, as well as some diamond sharp lines:

> A good part of the art of self-defence
> is to survive what we are learning.
> Memory is fragile
> Some doors simply close
> Entries and exits disappear
> Write, as some fish, for revelation.
> Every mother is delivered into fear.
> (Reprinted from *We Who Can Fly*)

The voice of the poems is personal, intimate, which is unusual in Adele's writing. There is an inconclusive, intense love story.

Another story lurked in those boxes: the rejection slips included in the files. Very few of these poems were published in her lifetime, or have been yet. After five years, she turned back to narrative forms, the long poem, and the brilliant "Goon of the Moon."

A third story lay interleaved between the poems: the first ideas for Adele's ambitious fiction, "Goon of the Moon and the Expendables," the gathering of themes, images, characters. This turned into my own essay.

As contributions came in, I could see how loved Adele had been. There was a moving memoir by Joyce Marshall, an unforgettable, never-before-published poem by Anne Michaels, a wonderful memoir by Caroline Adderson. The pieces sparkled. The manuscript grew.

Then came the hard part. The book was complete enough to query publishers, but it was unclassifiable — too literary for an academic book, too academic for a trade book. Some publishers liked the idea, but no one wanted the manuscript. It was bad enough getting rejection slips for myself, but what if I had to tell all my contributors — and Tamara — that I couldn't get the book published?

Rachel Wyatt thought it appropriate for Adele that I was finding the book so hard to place (I didn't tell her it was also all too appropriate for me). She said, supportively, that she could see the cover. "What does it look like?" I asked tentatively, but I could see it too: Sandra Rutenberg's previously unpublished photograph of Adele with her mother's dolls.

After I had approached thirty publishers, some with query letters, some with excerpts, some with the entire manuscript, I ran into Gary Geddes, now a successful poet and professor of creative writing at Concordia University. He suggested that I send the book to his wife, Jan, the publisher of Cormorant Books, which he had founded.

I did send Jan the manuscript in the summer of 1996 and didn't hear from her until December, when she wrote, explaining that Cormorant had almost folded but had negotiated a deal to continue under Stoddart's umbrella — she accepted the book.

As I walked through the winter streets, I could almost hear angels, or maybe just trees, singing. Adele would be honoured; the book wouldn't die. A door had opened that I'd thought would be forever closed.

After ten months of copy reading, revising, proofreading, arranging the pictures, and tracking down the people in the pictures, I held a copy of *We Who Can Fly: Poems, Essays and Memories in Honour of Adele Wiseman* in my hand. Sandra Rutenberg's photograph of Adele made a fine cover. The next morning, I flew to Banff for the book's first launch. There would be others in Kingston, Toronto, Windsor, and London. The next spring, *We Who Can Fly* was honoured with the Betty and Morris Aaron prize for Best Scholarship on a Canadian Subject at the Jewish Book Awards in Toronto.

—

CODA 2001. My second "first book" had mystic origins: I had written a story inspired by a woman in a tarot workshop, who e-mailed our group asking what it meant that she kept getting the Moon Card in her readings.

Many friends liked the story; some from Banff had workshopped it, but it too kept piling up rejection slips. With the encouragement of Kellye

Crockett, one of Kingston's best psychics, I decided to publish it myself. Cheryl Pelow, a Kingston artist who does tarot herself and specializes in mythic, magical pictures, did paintings and line drawings that perfectly matched the text. The next few months rolled by in a flurry of meetings with Cheryl and the book's designer, David Stone. Thanks to my experience with the Adele book, I knew the stages that come between manuscript and printed pages.

Self-publishing is quick! *The Moon Card* was born May 11, 2001. Two friends gave the launch, their home filled with friends, flowers, delicious food, and celebratory effervescence. Kellye came with her belly-dancing troupe, the Veils of Isis (who appear in the story). They shimmered as they danced in praise of the Divine Feminine. Cheryl and I felt we'd given birth to an exceptionally beautiful child. I couldn't imagine being happier.

A launch is just a beginning. Even a self-published chapbook needs nurturing: I contacted newspapers, placed it in bookstores, eventually sent it to the National Library. Cheryl also promoted the book.

With both books, the challenge for me was not so much nurturing them after they appeared as navigating the long, rocky path that led to publication. But there's a satisfaction at having managed rocky paths and looking back at the view. I take a swig from my metaphysical water bottle and start to consider sending out a third book.

Round Trip

WHEN I STARTED to write *The Embrace*, my motivations were many. To capture the experience of my parents' generation: flight from homeland, displacement, and loss of country, a pivotal experience that shaped both their generation and mine, and could not be allowed to vanish. To write honestly, for the exile community of my youth was thick with a sticky nostalgia. If I am totally honest, I felt aggrieved at "being Lithuanian"; at having to attend Saturday school; to maintain language, culture, and customs; to help keep another country alive. My book was an attempt to say to Canadian friends, who had no such concerns and whose lives seemed so easy and carefree, look what life is like for us. We don't have your lightheartedness, your freedom. We are shackled to obligation and duty, tied to the past and to another place. I wanted to come to grips with a dream handed down by my parents and grandparents, and denied by a Communist reality. I wanted to understand Lithuania's hold on my life.

Like all writers, I hoped for the preconceived path to Canadian literary success. A review in a mainstream newspaper, readings, a literary prize. None of that happened. Instead, the book cut its own path through the world.

SANTARA-SVIESA is a liberal cultural organization that concerns itself with Lithuanian history, art, literature, aesthetics, and economics. In Chicago, home to the largest gathering of Lithuanians outside of Lithuania, there is a chapter. Here, *The Embrace* found a warm home. They translated it into Lithuanian. Then, a Vilnius publisher published the book in Lithuania. This led to an invitation to the Vilnius Book Fair, a book launch, radio interviews, and invitations to speak at the universities in Vilnius and Kaunas.

To go to Lithuania is no small thing. In fact, it is emotionally overwhelming. It was not my first visit, but I was going alone. The first hurdle is language. Mine, learned from my parents and grandparents, is stuck in 1944. Next come the customs and culture. This is not casual Canada, but a European country, ancient and formal. I was afraid of my own ignorance, and of making faux pas. My hosts were the most welcoming of people. If they were taken aback or amused by my actions or words, they were far too polite to let it show.

The work was exhausting and exhilarating. The stimulation of shifting back into the language of childhood, and of being met on all sides by history and culture, kept me awake at night. I was far too alive to sleep. And I didn't want to miss a thing.

One evening, at dusk, I was waiting in the hotel lobby for a woman to deliver a video tape to take back to a friend in Canada. It is still our custom to ask travellers to carry goods between our countries, as if the days of samizdat are not really over, as if the care accompanying hand-passed items still lingers. Our business transacted, the woman made ready to leave. Before going, she said, "Why aren't you out in the streets? It's Uzgavenes. Go out and join the people."

—

UZGAVENES is the Lithuanian equivalent of Shrovetide, a season of merrymaking before Lent, a carnival owing as much to paganism as to Christianity. At dusk, people don costumes, dressing as evil spirits, demons, or traditional characters, then fill the streets in a party mood. A drama is performed outdoors to say goodbye to winter and to welcome spring. "More," a symbol of the clash between winter and spring, is wheeled about in a cart. A flail in one hand, a broom in the other, she is unable to make up her mind whether to continue flailing last year's harvest or to start sweeping the yard for spring cleaning. An effigy, she is burned after dark.

In the middle of this crowd, pellets of comprehension began to hit me. This was not a church basement in Toronto, the hermetically sealed environment of exile. These were city streets, teeming with the old, the middle-aged, and the young, parents with children perched on their shoulders, laughing teenagers, loving couples. This was not culture interrupted by displacement, loyally maintained in a different place, but, inevitably, artificially recreated. This was living culture, a simple continuation of customs, re-enacted year after year, the past becoming the present. This was not obligation and duty, but happiness.

And I thought, how will I explain this to my sister back in Toronto? How could a diaspora community possibly recreate Uzgavenes? It could not. At best, enacted on a church basement stage, it could only rekindle the memories of those who had once lived such an event. To the rest of us, re-creation could only be approximation. Context is impossible to convey. This is both painful and sad, for in the history of displacement and lost homeland, context is everything.

Diaspora and homeland are not equivalent. Diaspora is homeland out of context. My parents grew up in homeland. I did not. If my family told many stories, if they upheld teaching of language, culture, and customs — and I was lucky they did — there was just as much they could not convey, a knowledge they didn't know they had, a life context impossible to pass along.

The Embrace gave me something that history had denied. It gave me my own connection with Lithuania. Connection no longer mediated through family, but personal; no longer merely personal, but professional; no longer communal, but private; no longer dream, but reality; no longer imposed, but desired. Finally, Lithuania and I met. It was love at first sight. And the place became mine, too.

Fifty Cents a Copy

AT THE BEGINNING OF May 1976, Matt Cohen and I drove from Edmonton to Toronto in his new truck: a second-hand Japanese pickup. On account of the reconditioned engine, we took it slow: five days. We'd both just spent nine months at the University of Alberta, Matt as the university's first writer-in-residence, me as a new assistant professor in the English department. The previous fall, after I took him a poem, we'd become friends, but we'd never talked for five days straight. At the age of twenty-nine, I was a published poet and failed novelist. In my twenties I'd written three unpublishable novels and a Ph.D. on Bishop Berkeley. That year I'd put Matt's *The Disinherited* on my Canadian literature course, but the book of his that had knocked me out when I read it the year before in the British Library (where Canadian literature, like Canada, seemed a very long way away) was his first collection of stories, *Columbus and the Fat Lady*. It had never occurred to me to write short stories — it would be poetry, novels, or nothing — but after five days headlocked with Matt, I climbed out of his truck determined to try. The next day, at a card table in my parents' rec room, I started in.

Over the next four years I wrote about two dozen stories. When I'd finished a few, I'd mail them to Matt, who'd send me feedback, which often as not ended with the beautiful, amazing words "Send more stories." I knew at the time how generous this was, I didn't know how rare. I sent him everything I wrote.

One day Matt mentioned that Coach House Press wanted him to edit some fiction.

"You should edit a collection of my stories," I said immediately and immediately received one of his infinitely skeptical looks.

A few weeks later, he told me to send him all my best stuff. I did this, and the next spring we met at his cabin and chose twelve stories, which he arranged in a grid on the floor. In ten minutes we had the order. He didn't like my title, "The King of Germany," from an obscene poem about Mickey Mouse, which I wanted as my epigraph. He'd already suggested "Famous Players" as a better title for the last story in the collection, and this, he said, would also do for the book. I agreed. Nobody liked "The King of Germany."

The cover design for *Famous Players* was done by the greatly talented Gordon Robertson. Gordon's concept was a marquee-style title in red and black on a light blue background, with the bottom right-hand corner looking as if it was peeling back to reveal ... the author. The author, however, was uncomfortable with appearing on the cover of his own book, and said so to Matt, who must have agreed. The first story in *Famous Players*, "Life with the Prime Minister," treats a Trudeau-like politician as a famous player, and it happened that Coach House had a picture of Diefenbaker that they'd altered to give him big Hollywood shades, so Diefenbaker in shades became the famous player revealed by the peeling corner.

Notwithstanding my shyness about appearing on the front cover, for the author photo on the back I wanted myself bare-chested, like Michael Ondaatje on the back of *The Collected Works of Billy the Kid*, but Matt assured me that authors should never appear naked in their author photos. Instead Coach House went with one of me looking very stoned. For the back jacket copy, Matt wrote something wonderfully Cohenesque like, "Although Greg Hollingshead's characters do everything they can to avoid meeting each other, they don't always succeed." This characterization of my brilliant stories I felt was too flip, so I myself provided something cringe-inducing. If I mention that it included the words "unforgettable" and "country of the heart," you will know what I mean.

Coach House is famous for its handsome books, and *Famous Players* is a handsome book. But Coach House in those days was never really into sales and marketing. The founder and publisher, Stan Bevington, used to say that an author should think of his book as a fine calling card — as opposed, presumably, to a vulgar object of mass production. My publicity tour was a half-day walk to three Toronto bookstores — Pages, Longhouse, and the Bob Miller Bookroom — in the company of a hostile publicist, who as we trudged the baking streets directed my attention to a few of the many infelicities and "factual errors" that riddled my stories. The woman at Bob Miller was polite enough, though cool, and cast a jaded eye on me; the woman at Longhouse — who was not one of the owners — was downright insulting. Ignoring me, she asked the publicist, "So who've you dragged in today?" Only Marc Glassman, owner of Pages, was friendly. We sat in the back room while he and the publicist had a conversation that I couldn't follow.

Ken Adachi in the *Toronto Star*, Anne Collins in *Maclean's*, and an English professor named Terrence Craig in an Australian literary review gave *Famous Players* excellent reviews, but for the most part the book was ignored. Dennis Duffy reviewed it together with David Young's *Incognito* in the *Globe and Mail* under the title, " Wordy games." The next day David Young pied Duffy at a statue unveiling in Toronto. When *Famous Players* was shortlisted for the Alberta short fiction prize, Merna Summers, accepting the prize for her story collection *Calling Home*, helpfully advised me that as a writer I'd better get used to disappointment.

And so *Famous Players* quietly died. Who knows how many it sold? Probably around a thousand. I know Matt got Coach House to print extra covers in case it took off, but it never did.

Sometime in the early 1990s, I was making one of my annual visits to the Toronto bookstore This Ain't the Rosedale Library, where the co-owner, Charlie Huisken, who was always friendly, on this day greeted me with particular enthusiasm. I must really be selling, I thought. "Back here, Greg," he said. "I want to show you something," and leading me into a room filled with boxes, he explained that Coach House had let a lease expire on a basement full of their books, which the owner intended to destroy, so he'd gone in and rescued as many as he could. He was now looking into shipping them to China or somewhere, anywhere, that would take them. He pointed at a ten-foot stack of boxes of *Famous Players*. "So how many do you want?"

I took two boxes of forty at fifty cents a copy. As I carried them to the car, one on each hip, I thought: Books on quality paper sure are heavy. I thought: It was nice of Charlie to give me a good deal. I thought: I wonder how many actual calling cards you could buy for forty dollars. I thought: Is this really what it's going to be like?

Write of

Passage

I WAS RECENTLY at a dinner party where people were relating how poor they'd once been. A competition in remembered suffering. The winner was a boy whose mother had been a heroin addict. When he was a child, they'd lived in a dumpster in L.A. until social services took him away.

It doesn't work, splashing wine into a glass and conjuring up the hungry days. Too safe. Too indulgent. Too far away now from what it really felt like then. Once you move from wanting into having you cease to understand what it was you wanted. That's how I feel about being published. I can't remember it properly.

My first book came out over sixteen years ago and I'd be lying if I said I knew how I felt when I lifted the first copies out of the shipping box. Probably a mix of pride and relief and a certain measure of emptiness. Getting published is a marker, a validation, something to swim toward in this stormy, stormy sea. But once you get there it will be somewhere further out that you'll want to go. It's good that we're fickle beings because that's how we survive our lives and our choices. That's how we survive ourselves.

Being published has allowed me to believe in what I do, and who I am. It has changed the question at parties from, "Why haven't I heard of you?" to "Why does your name sound familiar?" And most importantly, it has enabled a relationship between writer and reader, a relationship I am fiercely grateful for.

It's a good thing I did get published because I hadn't left myself many other options. I didn't go to university. I worked pumping gas and washing cars. If I had never been published, I wouldn't have attended that dinner party. I'd have washed the special edition SUV of someone on their way to that dinner. And I'm sure they wouldn't have given me a tip for taking extra care in wiping down the running boards. I'm sure of that.

The
Words
You Eat

THE ADVANCE IS SETTLED with an expensive, but not fancy, lunch. We are eating it. Some we are consuming as scotch and a punchy Rioja. Some more — whichever way the imbalance must unburden itself — is repayment for that other thing, and also a loan on an unrelated miscellaneous promise and/or adventure. Actually, it's difficult to remember right now *what* this lunch is payment for, just that the publisher is getting the tab, and now I am writing the book. As I walk with the publisher — *my* publisher — to smoke an après steak shisha that will seal the deal, one thought I have is: I am maybe not making out like a bandit here. Another thought: Maybe I am making out like a bandit here. I pay for the shisha so there will be no hard feelings.

There is one awkward moment, when the (self-congratulatory) conversation (somehow) strays to structure and theme (and also topic). What's this book about? Do I have a title yet? I do. But I cannot possibly share it — not yet — because, it's one of those titles. Yes, abstract and intuitive, it's kind of — it's . . . trust me, it's *THERE*.

And the curse? (I'd forgotten all about the curse.)

Yes, I *have* been working hard on the curse.

Like a motherfucking dog, that's how hard. You saw some — *remember?* — at Christmas. Yah . . . that's going to be part of the book. Except not REALLY part. More like, it's a-a-a, a wry description, and also the, you know (and I cough here) "immunity protocol." Actually, you could say the curse *is* more of a *level*. In fact, you could say it *is* a level. The inner, inner, inner level. Inside the inner, inner level.

Still being written? I think logically it has to be *solved* before it can be written. I — *we* can't inflict things we don't know on the reader. Not even accidentally. These are *our* readers. We love these fucking rea —

How am I writing the curse?

I am writing it very, very carefully. I *could* "explain it," but then what would be the point of writing it? This is *why* we're writing it — because it can't be articulated. *This* is what your advance will cover. We'll have to ship it with coffee beans, that's one thing I do know. How come? *GOD — this steak's done PERFECTLY!*

Mmmm, it is. You like my suit? I'm wearing it for negotiating leverage.

Around us, suits that have been ironed are working out million dollar oil and land contracts using a less poetic vernacular. Their contracts are not pure, though. We're picking up the slack for all humanity right now.

—

AND MANY (MANY) MONTHS later my book is delivered. It's a two-volume vest pocket job — a form made popular at the turn of the twentieth century by Thomas Mosher and Frederic W. Goudy. At one point it had been a four- *and* seven-volume vest pocket job, structured around the seasons or days of the week (and also as a choose your own adventure, a Cortazaresque Calvinoesque choose your own adventure — *so* esque). The publisher praises my "randomness of thought" in an interview with a small press magazine. According to the magazine, the reading experience is "enhanced by fine paper, good workmanship and an unassuming and quiet typographic elegance." And it is.

The dimensions — the book is in my fingers for the first time — are 6 ½ by 4 ¾ inches. It is hand-stitched. The cover is constructed of Iwahada Namari paper. I hadn't realized it before, but I *love* Iwahada Namari paper. My book costs seventy-five Canadian dollars. This is a fair price given the materials, given its sheer beauty, given the fact that the craftsmanship has eclipsed the text itself. I wonder, though, if this price doesn't exclude some readers. For instance, I cannot afford to buy my own book. Fortunately, some copies — either three or four — are included *on top of* the very expensive lunch, because my publisher is maybe a worse negotiator than I am.[1] These are very special editions – one is sewn inside a map of Sarawak, Malaysia. (I am not kidding.)

It's worth noting that I receive this advance copy in Nicosia, the capital of Cyprus, where I am making a documentary. I promptly turn it over — after just holding it for a few minutes, the first copy of my first book — as a wedding gift to an old friend, whose nuptials will take place the next day. I do not read it before turning it over (for fear of screwing up the curse, and also for fear of depriving my friend of the joyous moment of cracking its twin spines). Everyone else at the wedding gives them envelopes stuffed with Cypriot pounds. Again, I'm picking up the universe's slack.

The second advance copy arrives at my apartment in Barcelona a month later. It is called *Towards An Erratic State*. I am struck by the title. There is a play on words there. What does it *mean*? There is a synopsis: "In the days between his release from the Borneo Psychiatric Hospital, and current disappearance, the convicted murderer and Chinese eclectic Thomas Tse penned a peculiar justification for our current state. Four years ago his text was discovered and translated by a Canadian missionary living in Kuching. This evocative translation and notes are presented in 2 rare vest pocket volumes. *Towards An Erratic State* is crafted in the controversial tradition of 'cursed books.' It is offered to YOU, diligent reader, with an unprecedented protocol for immunity." Interesting. This is something *I* would read (a thought I have whenever I hold a book in my hand that I am about to actually read).

And I begin to read.

As I read, I realize that my brain is a sentence ahead of my eyes. This is because I know every sentence by heart. Every word is in place. So I stop reading. I put on a CD (appropriately, it is a CD I was given in exchange for writing the liner notes). I spend the afternoon drinking and touching both volumes of *Towards An Erratic State*. Once I have memorized the ISBN, I go to work. I happen to be working for/out of one of those gnarly caves in the rabbit warren that constitutes Barri Gòtic in Barcelona. A girl named Sabine commissions poems from me, which she promptly turns into decor. In exchange, I get big chunks of Camembert, a slice of quiche, and a bottle of

Bordeaux, also the region where she's from. She brings out cake until I feel too guilty to eat any more (even though I am somehow still hungry) and I quickly finish my poem, leaving it under the base of the empty glass, then sneaking out the moment she bends behind the bar. Like an Australian leaving a bad tip.

While I am the reigning poet at Sabine's café, I am also e-mailing back and forth, somewhat timidly, with a publisher in Canada about an advance of *thousands* of dollars. Royalties, translation rights, book club rights, all kinds of rights and promises are on the table. I've been working with an agent who feels the deal is too small. Also, he has just disappeared from the agency for — as another writer tells me — "not dotting his i's and crossing his t's." If I'd just write an entirely different book, he said to me before disappearing, I could expect a much sweeter deal. And then the i's. And t's.

The contract is twenty pages long. I want some lunch provisions put in, but don't know how to legally word it. "I will trade Danish paperback rights if we can work in a Monte Cristo and a bowl of mulligatawny." Otherwise, the contract pleases me. I think. The "release" is more than a year away. The "manuscript" (as it is being called) exists in a dozen notebooks stored with people like Sabine. So it's *basically* done. Yet, between writer and audience there is such a long distance.

I kill some time. I keep writing for Sabine. I read some stories in some different magazines. I have written these stories, and some of the sentences look vaguely familiar. I wait some months for the cheques. Sometimes/ often I phone to inquire as to the whereabouts of these cheques. And also the whereabouts of the cheque for the expenses. And why are these cheques bouncing? (I sometimes have to ask.)

This next part is maybe not obviously pertinent (but also this story isn't quite as obviously about first books anymore):

I used to live with a girl (when I was writing my first book), a nice girl who didn't mean much harm, but who'd sneak up and read over my shoulder when I was typing at my desk. Even when she began turning her head to the wall as she approached, going so far as to close her eyes once she'd crossed the visual threshold from which the screen could be perceived, tripping over books on the floor — she only wanted to ask how my day had gone — I would twist my body into an accusatory shield, as if the computer was meat I had just killed. She was a vegetarian. She took my hostility as a trust missing in our relationship, a lack of love. After she left, I read an interview with the writer Ron Carlson who said, "Good writing needs a kind of keeping." I cut the words right off the page. I taped them to the back of my chair. I was living miserably alone, though, so after a few days I stuck them to the fridge, next to a funny description clipped from *The Guardian* about William S. Burroughs's derangement, and as writer friends would fumble with the door, grabbing for another beer, I'd see them hone in on the quote and nod knowingly. *Fucking eh*, they'd think. Is there any other occupation so privately public?

But does that explain the little café? How does it explain eating and drinking the payment as the product comes out at exactly the same time, a kind of photosynthesis in the candlelight, the typeface the stroke of a pencil (always on good behaviour in the café), Sabine's other denizens sitting all around watching curiously and angrily, begging for an ending, for the author to leave, and Sabine the publisher to come and examine the page and put it on the counter for — for what reason? Just to publish? No. To understand the currency of what she herself sold.

From the same Ron Carlson interview — and I can't say that I'm this avid a fan beyond having had scissors in reach the day I happened to read the interview — the interviewer says, "One of my favorite Ron Carlson quips is: 'A writer is the person who has written today.' What have you written today?" And Carlson — and you can't help think that he's one of those guys who doesn't skip a beat — he says, "I wrote a page about why a person might logically close the barn door after the horse has fled." I guess this is what I wrote today. At a desk. On an empty stomach.

---

1. The true reward lay in the royalties: promised copies of every broadsheet, every book, and every miscellaneous package that Fox Run will produce. Ever.

JEANETTE LYNES

Confessions
of a Hotshot,
Show-Off,
Canuck
Prima Donna

The First Book and the Writing Workshop

I USED TO PORE OVER writing work-
shop brochures the way a child might devour the toy pages of a Christmas
catalogue, or a Canadian-in-winter might luxuriate over travel packages to
sunny destinations. The workshop offered, in addition to the obvious oppor-
tunity to write, a chance to travel, meet writers, shake off routine's shackles.
While the late-winter snow melted, workshop brochures arrived in the
mail like shining promises: Banff, Fredericton, Victoria, Sligo. Which one,
which one?

At workshops or writing retreats in San Miguel, Key West, Bronxville,
or Lumsden, I'd bond quickly and commiserate contentedly with other
poets: how many times our manuscripts had been rejected, which presses

had rejected them, which magazines had given us the slip. The big question was always, "Do you have a book?" We workshopistas usually had a number of poems published separately in journals or magazines, and a sort of cobbled-together thing we thought *might* be a manuscript, but we weren't sure. We'd swap angst, and any bits of inside information we thought we possessed. We'd encourage each other. We'd promise to keep in touch. We mostly wouldn't. Still, we felt a sense of community, however briefly.

We were a community bound together, in part by our status as have-nots — that is to say, "No, we did not have a book. We did not know if we would ever have a book." Most of the workshops I attended took place before my first collection of poems appeared in December 1999. That first book changed my life. As slender as that volume was, as flawed as the little orphan-poems in it might have been, they now had a permanent home, and I didn't have to keep worrying about losing them anymore. I confess I carried FB (First Book) around with me all the time and kept it on my night table so it would be the first thing I saw every morning. I don't think I was vain so much as incredulous; it seemed important to keep reminding myself it really existed.

The first post-book workshop I attended was held over a weekend in Key West, Florida. Little FB was, of course, in my suitcase (after all, the plane could crash, I wanted it with me). The people at the workshop were nice. They spoke in soft, slidey accents, played guitars, and drove Bentleys. One writer from Nebraska kept flashing her book around. Everyone said all the right, admiring, congratulatory things. One book might be tolerated — after all, the "have-nots" still greatly outnumbered the single "have." One book can remain an anomaly, more than one would begin, we were to discover, to tip the solidarity scales. I kept my mouth shut about my book until the last day. The margaritas began to flow in a balmy outdoor café, and perhaps the imminent winter I would soon again face loosened my tongue. I confessed to my fellow workshopistas that I had a book.

Big mistake. The conversation stopped. The announcement (I'd tried to make it humbly, I really had) threw Miss Nebraska flat on her Wal-Mart-shorts butt. Her expression conveyed that she didn't appreciate being dethroned as the sole book-published poet — especially by some upstart from north of the 49th parallel. Who wrote in Canada, anyway? She didn't know *anyone* wrote, up there. This was said as a joke, but one of those jokes with a bit too much tang. The margarita soured on my tongue. The others didn't appreciate my "holding back" — why hadn't I told them I had a book the moment I waltzed into the workshop? Just then, a doctor from Pensacola announced that he, too, had a book and our table, which had begun as a big, happy family — the Waltons, for crying out loud — split into the haves and have-nots. The very community I sought in a writing workshop was undermined. Everyone was just a bit too polite, formal. The poets without books were friendly, but there was a subtle distancing, and I felt like I'd let my friends down by having a book. Maybe Miss Nebraska had done the right thing by announcing it right away — though I secretly suspected more than one person had found this obnoxious.

That workshop taught me about the gap between the booked and the unbooked. I had, of course, experienced the gap from the have-not side, but experiencing it from the side of those with books was startling in terms of how much FB altered group dynamics.

The second post-book workshop I attended was an ambitious five-day event near New York City. Each day brought a flurry of drafts. Each night we hammered our fingers off in the computer lab at Sarah Lawrence College. We were in heaven. Again, I had FB in my dorm room and I typed happily into the night on my laptop, a plastic cup of amaretto at my side. The workshop included a student, open-mike reading. The only poems I had that I believed fit to be heard, at that point, were in my book. Now, wouldn't you think I'd have taken what I'd learned about disclosure at the first post-book workshop and applied it to this event? But the amaretto-nights drafts weren't ready, so I grabbed FB and read a couple of poems.

The next morning, I was greeted with the following words from another poet: "You bitch, you have a book." Wow. Good morning to you, too. The indignant woman's tone was genuinely accusing, and, well, jealous. The moment was not pretty. This time, I was thrown on *my* charity-shop-shorts butt. I'd become, overnight, a hotshot, show-off, Canuck prima donna. I said as many self-effacing things that I could to wiggle away from the charge of being a bitch with a book, but to no avail. The damning evidence was there, between the covers. I said it had taken five years for this one little book, but this didn't seem to make any difference. I was scarlet-lettered for the rest of the workshop. Several participants were actually much less friendly after I'd come forward with my book. Granted, I am over-sensitive, but a poet can tell when she's getting the cool shoulder.

"Who cares about a few cranky poets?" you're probably asking. But my interactions with other, more generous writers shifted too. Conversations tended to revolve less around the struggles of writing since, because I had a book, it must all be easy for me, no problem at all. And here's the part where I probably will sound like a bitch — because I had a you-know-what, I began to feel, ironically, less like a writer and more like an editor. Several poets from that workshop were still sending me poems to critique a year later.

The best workshop I attended was designed for "advanced" poets with a full-length manuscript-in-progress or a published book. There were five of us, all at similar levels. I had FB in embryo. This workshop truly was heaven, since the awkward dynamics mentioned above didn't exist. We knew putting a book together wasn't easy, that we'd been fortunate enough to have had a few supportive editors and sympathetic mentors. We also knew how hard we'd worked, and how obsessive we'd become in terms of our poetry. I don't mind doing some advertising for this wonderful event: the Sage Hill Poetry Colloquium in Saskatchewan. This proved to be the most comfortable space for a writer just on the verge of a first book, as I was. I've never wanted to endorse things that are hierarchical, but workshops organized around level of experience do seem to be the most fruitful and functional.

Where did I go from there? To the loner phase. The hermitage (near good coffee shops). The retreat. The colony. The trajectory went from wildly mongrel groups to more specialized groups to no group at all. The road to atomization saddens me somewhat. I miss the shared angst. I miss the laughter, the margaritas. I miss dancing in Saskatchewan. I still go to a couple of workshops a year in Maine. But I look at my watch. I try to offer encouraging insights. I will ultimately put workshops behind me, though one day I'd love to lead some — then they'd expect me to have a book. And they'd have to find other reasons to call me names.

Publishing
Oxygen

March 23 '97

Dear Linda,
Thank you very much for the Annabel Lyon stories. Can you please refresh my memory and tell me again who she is and any pertinent details. And could you put me in touch with her? I was interested in the stories and found they've stayed in my mind.

Would she be amenable to working further on a possible collection — writing further material, swapping weaker for stronger. That sort of process?

I much appreciate your commending people to me.

John.

Annabel —
FYI,
Linda

April 23 '97

Dear Annabel,
I do like your stories and I think we ought to start putting a book together. I don't quite know when we'd publish — probably in about two years given

the logjam. That sounds distant, I know, but by the time you're revised, rewritten, written new ones, it'll be on you fast. And all the small presses are in the same bind. If that's okay with you, let's just assume that you're now working towards a first book with PQ . . .

Best —

John

THESE TWO LETTERS (with the middle note appended to the back of the first letter on a bright green Post-it note) were how I learned my first book was to be published. Linda was Linda Svendsen, my master's thesis advisor at the University of British Columbia's creative writing program. John was John Metcalf, editor at the Porcupine's Quill, a small Ontario press. Linda had sent him a few of my stories, something she did for many of her graduating students, to see if he might be interested in an entire manuscript.

I don't remember receiving the first letter. In the intervening month I must have written to John myself and sent him more of my work; I don't remember doing that either. I do remember opening the second letter in my parents' kitchen and starting to cry, and having to pull myself together since I was teaching piano out of their basement at that time and had a student arriving any minute. When I think of publishing my first book, that moment of ambivalence is what comes immediately to mind.

My parents, I know, thought I was experiencing something like the emotions of a runner at the end of a long race: hopes held in for so long finally released, and all that. (In fact, to extend the metaphor a little further, the race wasn't over yet. I began the first of the stories for the book that was to become *Oxygen* in the fall of 1994; completed my thesis and graduated from UBC in the spring of 1996; received John's letter accepting my book in the spring of 1997; and saw the book hit store shelves in May of 2000 — five and a half years, all told.)

Certainly, I wasn't unhappy with the house that had accepted me. Porcupine's Quill made smart, snappy books by good writers on fine paper, and John was (is) an utter gentleman, passionate about good writing, who shared my tastes (Evelyn Waugh, Amy Hempel) and cared about the same things I did (style, style, style).

Certainly, too, I was relieved that my career as a fiction writer was finally underway, at however glacial a pace. I didn't want to teach piano from my parents' basement forever and, with a philosophy degree and a creative writing degree, I wasn't qualified to do much else.

But imagine something hovering and spinning and glittering in the air above your head, something like a constellation. Imagine tossing up a great net to catch that thing, only to have it fall out of the sky, rhythm destroyed, a handful of dull stones. That was what I was afraid would happen to the book that had previously existed only in my imagination.

Let me stress that this was a momentary reaction, a fault line that opened and closed again as the tectonic plates in my head adjusted to the new reality: my book would be published. As the months and years went by — 1997, 1998, 1999 — the machinery of that first book continued to wind and grind, slowly but surely. Working on the old stories and writing new ones was a deep pleasure and even a kind of sanctuary, for I made some missteps along the way: I started law school in 1997 and dropped out a year later (no time to write); started a novel in 1998 and gave it up for a failure in 2003 (educational, I still tell myself, through gritted teeth, educational). Y2K came and went, and my computer survived; a photographer friend of my father's graciously agreed to shoot the photo of a less-than-gracious, camera-shy author; we found a cover for the book, a beautiful Ray Mead painting, a red colour field with an abstract black shape at the bottom that was probably not meant to resemble a barbell, though thank you for asking. The fault line opened again, briefly, when Canada Post left a sticker on my door saying there was a parcel waiting for me at the post office in the 7-Eleven a few blocks away, and I saw the parcel had come from the Porcupine's Quill and knew it must contain the first copies of my finished book. I took the parcel home, put it in a cupboard, unopened, and left it there for many hours while I did other things.

I had not told many people that I had written a book. I had certainly not told my piano students or their parents, but one Saturday morning in May I was unceremoniously outed when a large photograph of me appeared alongside a review in *The Vancouver Sun*. Whatever respect my students might have had for me immediately vanished. We saw you in the paper, they said slyly, as though they had discovered a secret that gave them power over me forever. In a way I suppose they had. The older teenage girls and their mothers read the book, and (I got the feeling) didn't really know what to make of it. It had sex, and language, and depressed people watching TV. The younger kids (and a lot of their parents) couldn't understand why I was still teaching piano after my picture had been in the paper. A lot of these same parents would bring their kids to lessons week after week for years, and, while casually writing out the month's cheque, ask me what I did for a job. This, I would say, teaching piano. And they would say, no, but your *real* job. Imagine trying to explain the economics of fiction writing to these good people.

Meanwhile, as more reviews accompanied by more photographs came out, and my last shreds of credibility with my students were shot all to hell, John was phoning regularly to ask if I felt my life had changed yet. This was a common refrain of his: my book would come out and my "Life Would Change," in ways I could not possibly foresee. After a while the question grew irritating (forgive me, John). I was still teaching piano; I was still broke. But of course he was right. I've since published a second book, a collection of novellas called *The Best Thing for You*, and am working on a third. The piano stays closed these days, and "writer" is what I put on my tax returns now, though some years with more confidence than others.

Self-confidence is a funny thing. After *Oxygen* came out, I began to persuade myself not that the next book would be perfect, but that I was improving, slowly but steadily, step by tortoise step. I'm still not sure if this was a maturing process, a surrender, or a mere substitution of one fantasy for another. Children demand perfection (the happy ending, good beating evil, perfect love, the stringent moral purity of cartoons). Most philosophers outgrow their affection for Platonic ideals. I decided I would put away childish things and focus not on the shimmering golden goal but on the journey, the slow accumulation of wisdom and experience that would hopefully leach into my writing. Perhaps that, too, was the fantasy of a quite young artist.

Then again, maybe a part of me had given up. I was struggling with longer narratives — novellas, maybe a novel — and had realized I couldn't afford to spend all my time fiddling around with tricky-clever sentences. There were pages to amass, stories to plot. I told myself that high style and big structure were (for me, at least) incompatible, and that I would have to cultivate a quicker, cooler prose style if I was ever going to get to the end of something long. Of course, there are many beautifully stylish novels that put the lie to this notion, but I could not see how to accomplish one myself. The pure, head-out-the-window, tongue-flapping-in-the-wind joy I had felt writing the stories in *Oxygen* was gone. The novellas left me cautious, wary, and often frustrated.

It was during those darkest moments that I began to tell myself the following story: one day, many books and years hence — I pictured myself old, living alone, with a tired hip and an even shorter temper than I have now — I would write a book that was not perfect but very, very good, a book that would leave the bright dance of language aloft and intact. A gravely reduced ambition, perhaps. Most likely. I still hope it's true.

Houses

AT FIRST I didn't want to send out the manuscript. It was going to be buried like a dead pet. A pair of friends told me I was purely masochistic. I didn't argue. I did, after some encouragement, finally put together a query letter with a sample consisting of the collection's opening story. I sent out three such packages: one to a big, well-respected house; one to a not-so-big but well-respected house; one to a well-respected and significant small house. The big house was my first pick largely because they made such beautiful-looking books, and that's how I judged them, by the cover. I kept busy with some video games, books on meditation, and writing a short story with the burn-off energy from my collection. This little tale was a pale prose imitation of a black and white Swedish film featuring a stranded car and a bickering couple.

The first place to respond to my query was the big house. An editorial assistant left a message on both the phone and e-mail, saying she'd been going through the slush pile on the weekend and happened upon my story and wanted to see the rest of the manuscript. I waited three days to reply, partly out of disbelief and cowardice, but also naive arrogance. The editorial assistant was encouraging. We struck up an e-mail friendship. She kept me posted on my manuscript's progress through the necessary hallways and stairways in the big house. It was an exciting but excruciating ride. Meanwhile, the not-so-big house asked to see my manuscript. I had yet to hear from the small house.

I was sleeping in when I got the next call from the big house. My room-mate shouted through the door ... it's an editor from the big house and she's pretty sure you'll want to call her back! I said, really, and bundled myself under the covers. When I finally did call the big house back, I probably didn't sound very excited, especially when the editor made me an offer, because I was simply stunned. Not by the amount, it was quite modest, but mostly due to the fact that the book was a fiction collection and not the more lucrative novel format. The big house couldn't pay me as much as the novelists got, the editor said. Two days after this fateful phone call, the not-so-big house e-mailed me to say they weren't going to make an offer. Next I approached an agent who was very helpful, offering some advice. I didn't end up signing on with an agent, however. I figured I'd done all the hard work already.

Things to which I said no: a two-book deal; calling my book a novel; adding the word "Dreams" to the title.

When I went to visit the big house, a very large and new and even beau-tiful office in a steel and concrete and glass building in a bustling city, I was introduced to the person in charge of contracts, who invited me to sit down across from her large desk and read the standard contract the big house had prepared for me. It was a big, seamless, airtight, legal document. Weighing me down with some nice free hardcover books, she encouraged me to sign the contract before I left the building.

The big house wanted an option on my next book wherein I had to produce an entire manuscript before they'd consider having first right of refusal.

The big house was an imprint of a bigger house, which in turn was a Canadian subsidiary of an American house, which was part of a huge multi-national conglomerate based far, far away. This big picture had eluded me when I sent out my manuscript and, to be honest, it wasn't something with which I was completely comfortable afterwards. Still, I made my decision and told myself and others that I was fortunate. The people at the big house were a pleasure to work with. My editor was professional, warm yet efficient, and possessed an uncanny radar for character believability and continuity. All this despite the possibility that she had too many books on the go. (Maybe mine was the one too many, since it was apparently the last one to be signed for the following spring.) I thought the cover art for the book was perfect: a blurred photographic image where the interplay of light, colour, and movement was visceral yet melancholy. I was truly very fortunate to be in a house that took such care, and of course had the resources, to make such great-looking books.

The small house never replied to my query letter. However, as my editor at the big house told me, to be fair, many small houses neither have the resources, employees, nor time to get to unsolicited manuscript submissions as quickly as the big houses. I only heard from the small house after a friend of mine had talked to its editor and mentioned I got an offer from the big house. The editor at the small house then e-mailed me, saying my manuscript had been under consideration there for some time and she was shocked I hadn't kept her posted of the latest developments. But, of course, the small house never had my manuscript, just a query letter. Small assaults on the truth notwithstanding, I'd send to the small house again, after first being refused by the big house.

The book launch was in a huge bookstore, part of a chain that was barely Canadian-owned, if at all, and did its damnedest to try to convince us otherwise. It was a fancy affair involving other young writers on the spring list. We had to pose for pictures, and stand around and chat and act like we were best buddies. I spent most of the evening talking to some friends in the corner and then got drunk, thereby sabotaging my editor's well-meaning attempt to get the sales reps interested in me and my book.

Reviews of the book were generally good (small-run papers) to mixed (national). One busy reviewer declared that my stories were too long. One "bad" reviewer was ticked off that I'd live in the small town named in the book (which I hadn't) and then move away and write a whole book trashing it. One day I spoke to a young journalist from a national paper that's more American than Canadian, only to find later that what I thought was a good interview had been chucked into a piece of fluff about first-time authors. In a nutshell, the article suggested that people of my ilk were signed by big houses based on their youth and looks. The next week, a letter appeared in the paper, ridiculing the idea that I would be signed on my looks. Hey, it was press. As for my only television appearance, all I can say is that I was glad the talk show's phone-in guest was my roommate and that nobody else on the show knew at the time. We had a nice chat and complimented each other's work, with which we were quite familiar.

DON McKAY

By
Mistake

BACK IN THE 1970s, during the early days
of Brick Books (in fact so early it was then called Nairn Press), we brought
out a book by me called *Lependu*. Its inspiration and chief character was
Cornelius Burley, the first man to be hanged in London, Ontario, one half
of whose skull was on view in Eldon House, a local museum and stately
home. Burley's story offered a veritable curio shop of sensational details:
first he was hanged twice, the rope having broken on the first attempt; then
his skull was hollowed out and used by a famous phrenologist named
Fowler to prove that Burley must have been, on sound phrenological evidence,
innocent; and on top of this there was the simple shock of this half skull
displayed in Eldon House alongside trophies collected in colonial Africa —
wildebeest, lion, warthog, keidu, and Thompson's gazelle. (It has since been
removed, I believe, and interred with the rest of Cornelius Burley in Michigan.)
This was pretty rich stuff to surface in a city whose contemporary reputation rested on an insurance company and a business school, and it acted as a
shot of pure adrenalin to the imagination. By the time I'd finished with it,
and it with me, Burley had modulated and transmogrified in all directions,
most notably into a trickster named Lependu, whose presence could be felt
throughout the city fostering all manner of mischief and sly *memento mori*.

All that is prelude to the scene of the book's publication, which was our
kitchen. In those days, we Brick types did all the design, layout, and paste-up

ourselves, meaning that Stan Dragland and Jean McKay were to be found hovering over the two homemade light boards making fine adjustments to the delicate waxed sheets of poetry that had come from the printers, while I checked them against the proofs and gofered, and a noisy, cheerful (this is memory, remember) rabble of kids and dogs swirled through the kitchen and up the back stairs, getting into God knows what. This was hands-on. This was amateur in the best sense. Maybe every book of poems should be required to risk a kitchen on its way to that particular, exquisite room of its own.

Anyhow, it was quite a while later — months or maybe years — when I noticed that, with *Lependu*, we had accomplished a bibliographical rarity: a book whose author's name does not appear on its title page. Well, I say "we," when it's really me, as both proofreader and author, who must shoulder the blame. Or, as I now think, be credited with a lapse of unconscious genius. I mean, what better way for the trickster to make his presence felt than by excising the name of the callow poet who summoned him to these pages? To quote from one of them:

> Scales and exercises, étude, séance,
> technical pursuit until
> you catch him by mistake.

Sorcerer's apprentice, c'est moi.

Pumpkin and Clogs

MY WRITING GROUP kept expecting me to quit. "I can't figure out why you don't quit," one of them actually said. Not that they were pushing me out. It was just tradition — stay with the group until you get a book contract, then quit. We had lost a few members over the years that way. So now that *A Litany in Time of Plague* was going to be published, why was I still hanging around?

Looking back over the diary I kept during that pre-publication period, I suspect inertia had a lot to do with it. Life tends, astonishingly, to go on. Less than a month after recording "The News" ("I have a book coming out, a book coming out, a book coming out!"), I was griping and glooming about all the usual garbage: "I hate the summer. Everyone's away. I wander the stores, buy things I don't need, read too many Ruth Rendells one after another, see too many movies, eat too much, and gain weight. At the moment, I'm fat, lonely, piggishly behind in my housework, dubious in my faith, and semiblocked as a writer."

A book contract, I was learning, waves no wands and solves no problems. The transformation is less in ourselves than in the way others perceive us. They see a coach and glass slippers; we know it's all still a pumpkin and clogs.

My slim collection had been accepted by the Porcupine's Quill Press on the condition that I beef it up with at least three more stories. Fiction on demand, in other words. Fiction to deadline. And the blank page every bit as blank as ever. "I have four hugely begun stories piled on my desk," I moaned in those early days. "I have a computer to buy; I may or may not be on the Journey Prize short list; I may or may not win the Journey Prize; I may or may not ever have a fresh idea in my head again instead of old stuff revised or new stuff that turns out to be a dead end." Then, a week later, a little bit of serenity: "I've learned something, for about the fiftieth time. The joy of writing is in the writing itself, not in contracts or prizes or anything else that depends on others' approval."

The trouble with real-life epiphanies, though, as opposed to the ones that happen in the movies, is that there's no finality, no swell of music and roll of credits. According to my diary, it was during this pre-publication period that I deliberately, and with eerie calm, threw my mug at a filing cabinet at work. I even warned everybody beforehand. Then, bam! The mug remained intact, but the metal file drawer still bears a dent. And I somehow doubt that the "joy of writing" was the immediate cause.

On Christmas Day, 1993, with months still to go and stories yet to finish before I would hold that first book in my hand, I wrote: " The head is emerging. What a strange, wonderful, painful, sad, happy time this has been. I've been selfish, virtually a recluse, turning down invitations. Well, I suspect most birthing mothers are not exactly party girls. Christmas Eve Mass last night. Somehow, through all the clutter and caterwauling of the family service, something comes through, in the shape of the wafer in the mouth, the tang of the wine."

That tang comes and goes, however, in art as much as in religion. On January 31, 1994, I wrote, "My book is finished. *A Litany in Time of Plague* goes in the mail to [editor] John Metcalf tonight or tomorrow. I feel safely delivered, grateful and a little sad." Then, a few weeks later, for reasons that entirely escape me now, I was quoting from Psalm 88: " You have plunged me into the lowest abyss; into the darkest regions of the depths ... You have removed my friends from me and made me utterly loathsome to them. I am shut in with no escape; my eyes are dim with anguish."

What the hell was *that* about? Seasonal Affective Disorder? PMS? I really hadn't expected the bustle and sudden exposure of publication,

inimical as it is to the quiet furtiveness of writing, to get to me. My background and training are in the theatre. Stage productions are born of a mix
of hysterics and rage, and there is no pressure like an audience arriving at
eight. So I had thought that I would be totally unaffected by the business
end of producing a book. But my diary entries for the two months leading
up to the launch are a study in ambivalence.

September 16, 1994: "I have been through galleys and vandykes of
Litany ... I'm to read in Ottawa at the National Library on October 27 and at
the Rivoli in Toronto on November 2." October 4: "A long period of not
writing creatively. Just reading, organizing, preparing for the launch. I've
booked my train tickets and hotel, and feel terribly grown up." October 9:
"The thing to do is *work*. Play writer. Like in the old days. Write for the
sake of writing. Write the way you did before you had no hope of publication. I've got to get it back. I've got to drop all this silly shit and get it back."
October 15: "The books arrived yesterday. They're beautiful. They look
like the season. The front cover is wild — reds and yellows and a menacing
blue. The back cover is pale salmon — a surprise." October 24: "I've discovered I love to write, but hate being a writer. Writing brings out the best in
me; *being* a writer, the worst."

But as somebody once said, all shall be well, and all shall be well, and all
manner of thing shall be well. Ten years have passed. My third book was
published three years ago, and I'm hard at work on my fourth. Sometimes
I'm into my second cup of morning coffee before I remember that fact. No,
I'm not blasé. But experience does take the edge off. When my second book
came out, I fretted about my comparative lack of excitement, actually missed
the mood swings that greeted the first. Because as my diary testifies, there's
nothing like the first.

October 26, 1994: "Two years ago, everything I wanted was what I have
today. How our expectations rise. In four hours, I'll be on the train." Later
that day: "I'm here [in Ottawa]. I phoned John about the reading tomorrow,
then took a walk and had supper in the William Street Café ... I feel so free,
so full of beginnings. In the café I sat across from a young man with a blonde
goatee, who was scribbling madly in a notebook. It was all exactly what I
wanted."

The next day: "It all went perfectly. I read very well, and sold about 22
books, which I'm told is excellent ... I'm a writer!" And a week later, in

Toronto: "My whole life was there last night at the Rivoli. People from my church. People from work. Old friends. Family. My writing group, members past and present … All the pieces came together … I'm very tired. And I'm very, very, blessed."

L O R I E   M I S E C K

A Ritual
for Yes

MY FIRST BOOK, a book of poetry called *the blue not seen,* was published in the fall of 1997. Earlier that year the publisher, Rowan Books, had asked to read the manuscript and offered me a contract. There was one catch. They were publishing slimmer volumes of poetry and my manuscript registered in at one hundred and twenty pages, roughly double the page length that the press had intended on publishing. The first decision I had to make was that if I wanted the book published with the press, I would have to remove two of the four sections.

Before being published, *the blue not seen* was a manuscript about the death of my sister Betty, who died in 1986 at the age of 29; I was 25. It also included sections about being raised by an immigrant father and the implications of place and belonging, the birth of daughters and the birth of a new language, and being married to an immigrant, the way history repeats itself. In discussion with the press, we decided that the core strength lay in the two sections called "the blue not seen" and "you are here" and cut the two sections about immigration. With these sections gone, the manuscript became an intense examination of death and grief and birth.

I write from the marrow of my life. And it's in these bones where my language forms, and where an argument has ensued. It is this: though that great axiom, write what you know, was drilled into my head from primary school on, the idea of writing autobiographically seemed wrong. Writers should invent, not report. What I had yet to learn was that the invention was in the line, in the rhythm, in the sound, and that metaphor holds more emotional truth and wisdom for me than the facts of my life. Perhaps what should be added to that fateful advice about writing what you know is, it's not what you say, it's how you say it. I learned this as I learn most things — through the act of doing.

Early in my writing career and long before I was thinking about a manuscript, I sent four poems to a magazine on the west coast. Though certain they would publish the one about spring, I sent three others to "fatten the package." These three addressed the death of my sister and were, I believed, too personal in nature. Yet I included them and months later, to my surprise, I received a letter from the editor that stated they were publishing three poems, none of which paid homage to the return of light, a tulip, or a crocus. The editor had taken the time to write a personal note about the poems and encouraged me.

After publishing these poems, I continued to write, moved house, gave birth to a second daughter, looked for work, battled in relationships, made up in relationships, all the while taking rejections to heart and acceptances in stride. I continued to write about loss and longing. I continued to write about sisters, mothers, and daughters. I wrote about fathers and immigration. I continued. I wrote.

I could see a manuscript, what became *the blue not seen*, taking shape. I saw themes and motifs. I took advantage of writer-in-residence programs, creative writing classes, and workshops. I applied for a Canada Council grant, negotiated my time, and explored the language of unspeakable grief over the loss of a sister. I received the grant. I edited, I trashed, and wrote more.

On bleaker days, I grew obsessed with my lack of formal training and my despair over being unable to get beyond what I considered the personal. I did not possess an English or creative writing degree and to address this deficit, I created a self-directed and often highly intuitive course of reading. A gifted creative writing teacher introduced me to the work of Kristjana Gunnars, Di Brandt, Patrick Lane, Adrienne Rich, Virginia Woolf, Yehudia Amachai, and W. G. Sebald. I was stunned at the beauty of the work. When I read their poems or prose, I was captured and captivated and not once while I read did I wonder or care if the experience imparted in the work really happened to the writer.

I read essays and books on writing. Works like Tillie Olsen's *Silences*; *Language in Her Eye: Views on Writing and Gender*, and Janice Williamson's *Sounding Differences: Conversations with Seventeen Canadian Women Writers*. I was hungry for words and read everything I could find on poetics, particularly those who wrote what American poet Sharon Olds has called "apparently autobiographical."

It was during this time of discovery and manuscript shaping that I was shocked back into the hard reality of living. Another sister of mine, Sheila, died suddenly. On a bitterly cold morning in December, she was abducted from the parkade at her work, and was raped and murdered. Her body was found eleven days later.

My writing vanished into a waking nightmare of harsh images and rendered silence. But my reading didn't. Images and words of many fine writers kept me anchored in the world. Bertolt Brecht wrote, "In the dark times, will there also be singing? / Yes, there will be singing. / About the dark times."[1] Miguel Hernández, who died at the age of thirty-one in a Spanish prison, wrote, "I go in the dark, lit from within; does day exist? / Is this my grave, or the womb of my mother?"[2]

I realized that books at their finest harbour us against the sometimes wildly unpredictable waters that we call life. During those days when the world descended into winter and darkness, a dear friend arrived with a beautifully bound journal and a pen. She said, "Here, write this down to remember."

Though I barely remember applying, I was accepted for the Banff writing studio. Ten months later I went there, taking with me the then nameless *the blue not seen*. Rowan Books had asked to see the manuscript, and, though I had said I would send it, I had not yet done so. With a backdrop of bruised, icy mountains and unrelenting snow, I slept, ate, and worked odd hours, which I couldn't seem to afford myself at home. I wrote some new poems and cut others. I learned to understand more about silence and solitude. I learned that as a poet and as a reader of poetry, I had to be still and quiet to be moved. And in the between hours, another voice emerged, which I recorded in that beautifully bound journal. Fragments of sound that I jotted down were field notes for another manuscript, which would be published five years later as *A Promise of Salt*.

Before the launch of *the blue not seen*, I'd imagined myself clinking celebratory toasts to a job well done. Instead, I worried, and no more acute was the anxiety than when I was promoting the book and not reading from it. In one interview, the first question asked was if I thought one needed to suffer to create art. I don't remember what I answered; however, I do remember the opening sentence of the article, which read, "Lorie Miseck has suffered." All I could think of was Hester Prynne and her scarlet A, replaced in my case by the letter S. S for suffering. That unfortunate article set the tenor for the mortification I felt — the kind of nakedness reserved for nightmares.

I hid for days. I was horrified. Why I couldn't celebrate the book had more to do with not yet learning an essential lesson. I had always had a ritual for *no*, but never a ritual for *yes*. When no comes in the form of a large brown envelope, I hold it in my hand like a scale weighing its contents. The heavier the envelope, the heavier the no. If the no comes to me from a literary magazine where I've sent a few poems, I set aside an afternoon, fill it with all the rejections I've known. All the times I've been told to be quiet, all the lovers whose backs I've memorized as they walked away, and all the instances I've throbbed in shame like a thumb hit by a hammer or closed in a door.

I slowly sink into an afternoon like this as one would sink into a bath. I greet teachers who said I'd amount to nothing, and listen for the taunting voices that have followed me since childhood, voices that always know where I live. I wait until I am shrivelled, puckered like fingers that have been immersed in murky water too long. Then I step out and pull the plug on the drain. From practice, I know this will end. I will dry myself off and return to writing — that gentle space of birth and beginnings, where words have not yet learned about submissions and self-addressed stamped envelopes.

What about a ritual for yes? Though I've been pleased when poems have been published or broadcast, I've spent little time and very few afternoons reminding myself of other yeses. When the big yes came for my first book I was thrilled. But it wasn't long before I waded into new murky waters: Why did I write about this, why didn't I make it fiction? Why didn't I choose different material?

What is the relationship of content to language? I spent many nights reading texts, believing I was looking solely at the content. Other nights, reading the same texts, I believed I was looking solely at language. I thought I could separate content from language, like separating an egg. Like paint from the picture. Having a trained, detached eye crafts the material, but this condemnation of my own content stops me cold, and leaves me staring at a blank screen or a blank page.

I have tried the other way, to ignore the voice, and write about what I choose from my head. But sooner or later images appear like landmarks that lead me back to the content I've ignored. I can choose the language and shape, but my material chooses me. When writing about a charged emotional experience, such as a death in the family, the lines between the personal and public are blurred. If it is not to be disguised or transformed through fiction, then difficult questions must be asked and resolved. How does it, and how should it, differ from journal entries? Is the "I" me?

At the time my first book came out, I wish I had been in my body long enough to learn how to separate myself from the work. I know now that there is a moment when all the doubt and the internal noise of the critic falls away. It happens when I read aloud from my work. It is a moment of communication, of sharing the work with an audience, opening to, say, page twenty, or thirty-four, or five, and beginning to read aloud. It happens in the present moment, in the immediacy of the words where mercifully I, the writer, vanish, and the work remains. I regret not acknowledging my work and what I had accomplished. I received word via a news release that my book had been shortlisted for the Writers Guild of Alberta Henry Kreisel Award for Best First Book. I told my mother, husband, and only a few friends, and decided I would travel the three hours south to Calgary on my own for the ceremony. At the last minute, divine intervention arrived in the form of a babysitter and my husband came with me to the ceremony.

I look back at the person I was, so unsure of myself, so vulnerable and raw, carrying the intensity of emotion as I did in a recurring dream I had in junior high of arriving at school naked or partially clad. But these emotions had little to do with the poems in the first book; the poems were fine, set, fixed, and bound. These emotions had little to do with the writing as finished work, or the act of writing, but had everything to do with a writer learning to manage her writing life, and learning to separate and let go of the work that was finished. This was being accomplished sometimes gracefully, sometimes not, at a time of great personal pain. I think back then the writer in me knew there would be another book about a sister's death.

My second book, *A Promise of Salt,* was published by Coteau Books in 2002. A work of literary nonfiction, *A Promise* is a story told in poetic prose of a sister's longing. A monologue to a murdered sister, telling her what has happened since her death. The reaction to my first book helped prepare me for my second, which I knew would garner attention because of the public nature of Sheila's death. When the book came out, I decided that if I became full of anxiety and doubt, I would read aloud from the work rather than think about the work. That is, I would trust the words on the page over the multitude of my worries about this text being in the world. I believe the practice of reading the text aloud let the work stand and breathe on its own. I decided I could say no to interviews, and if I chose to do an interview, I did not have to read the interview afterward. I also had the choice of whether or not to read the reviews.

In the writing of *A Promise,* I went slowly. If it became too much, which it often did, I put it away. I returned to reading. Even now I find discussing the work much more difficult than reading from the work. When people ask me questions about my sister's murder, what it was like, I flounder and feel exhausted in coming up with a response. Yet when I read from *A Promise,* I feel grounded and sane. The book has structure and metaphor. Even now, when I consider sending out new work, I still have to remind myself how to take "me" out of my work, or my work out of "me." An exorcism of the ego. Yet when I'm creating new work, and the conditions are right, I step aside and let the writer write.

No matter what the genre — fiction, nonfiction, poetry — I believe facts are far less relevant than truth. Each time I pick up a book I suspend disbelief. What matters to me is the story or the evocation of the poem; the way language is used — its rhythm, its music, and how words can awaken compassion and provide a new way of seeing. And what I love in the act and art of creating is putting my ear to the earth, listening for the aches and joys, where the situation and facts are the small beats longing to lead me closer to the heart of truth.

1. Bertolt Brecht, in Carolyn Forché (ed.), *Against Forgetting, Twentieth Century Poetry of Witness* (New York: W.W. Norton & Company: 1993)
2. Miguel Hernández, "I go into the dark lit from within," in Carolyn Forché (ed.) *Against Forgetting, Twentieth Century Poetry of Witness* (New York: W.W. Norton & Company: 1993)

When in Doubt, Scream

AUTHOR'S NOTE: One way I survived the publication of my first novel was to keep a diary of my writing life. What follows is an excerpt from a particularly eventful day.

—

6:30 A.M.

My early-riser husband whispers in my ear that the newspaper profile I was interviewed for last week has been published this morning, and that the reporter called the protagonist of my novel "one of the most appealing heroines in current Canadian fiction."

I get out of bed to read the article and see what he hasn't told me: I look terrible in the accompanying photo — my eyes are puffy, my eyebrows out of control, my smile forced, my hair ragged. The brick wall I'm standing in front of looks excellent, though.

I also notice the piece contains no mention of tonight's reading at the Harbourfront Reading Series, which was sort of the point. Still. The article is positive, describes me as an up-and-comer, and quotes me sounding thoughtful on the whole race-identification issue (my book and I are not just about being a member of a visible minority).

I should be happy. I am happy.

—

10:20 A.M.
I drive out to the suburbs to tape a TV interview.

I expected (and dreaded) a studio taping, but I'm met at the security desk by a young woman named Stephanie who leads me to an office cubicle, and bids me sit in an ordinary office chair (behind which there is an atmospheric bookshelf — the apparent rationale for this location). Stephanie positions herself in a chair facing me. A man appears bearing a video camera and announces his intention to shoot me from over Stephanie's shoulder.

"Nice set-up you've got here," I say. "Very glamourous."

They both smile politely.

The cameraman attaches a microphone to my jacket, says, "Should I get a light for you, Stephanie?"

"Oh no," she says, "I won't be on-camera."

Guess I don't need a light.

Stephanie asks me the usual questions. I give the usual answers and am dismayed to find my voice shaking. Plus she keeps smiling at me in a way that makes me think she is signalling me to smile — like my mother does when I'm out in public wearing an expression which, in my mother's opinion, is either too surly, or unflattering to my facial planes. Every time Stephanie telegraphs me these wide smiles, I smile back, even when what I'm saying is not smile-worthy.

Stephanie wraps up the interview, shows me out, and says something incomprehensible about bumpers and clips and packaging. Also that she'll call to let me know when I'll be on. (She never calls; the interview never runs.)

I say, "Great! Thanks! It was fun!" despite the fact I was unlit, had a shaky voice, and smiled inappropriately.

I get into my car and scream.

—

1:00 P.M.

I prepare for the next big event of the day: my first live radio interview.

Alone in my study, I practice my interview answers for the nth time. I stumble on the "What's your novel about?" question. My rehearsed line is, "It's a romantic comedy about the deceiving nature of appearances," but all I seem able to say is, "It's about appearances," full stop.

Speaking of appearances, my hair has a tendency to droop at exactly the hour of tonight's Harbourfront reading. So, feeling not a little foolish, I wet down the droop-prone parts, and wipe off my makeup in preparation for a refix of both elements in a few hours. Ah, the life of the published author.

—

3:50 P.M.

I arrive early at the CBC building for the radio interview, which gives me time to go to the bathroom twice before I enter the studio. After I sign in, I'm directed to the waiting area, where I read a brochure about a recent Asian heritage arts festival and wonder if I should feel slighted or grateful for not having been asked to participate in it.

At 3:58, the producer appears and instructs me to join the program host, Katherine, at the "round table," after the 4:00 news begins. When I do, Katherine asks if anyone's going out for coffee. It's 4:02. I am slated to be on at 4:10. Should I offer to do the coffee run? Or maybe I could go pee again.

I put on my earphones and have my voice level tested by technicians on the other side of a glass panel. The news ends, Katherine announces the time and weather, says, "In a minute we're going to meet Toronto author Kim Moritsugu, author of *Looks Perfect*," and my stomach jumps up and down. "But first," she says, "we'll hear an old song called 'I Feel Pretty,' sung by, of all people, Little Richard."

I feel pretty, indeed. I take off my jacket. I extricate my skirt from under the wheels of the chair. I try to take deep healing breaths without appearing to do so. The song ends, Katherine comes back on the air and starts her intro on (gulp) me.

I answer her questions — the first set of non-generic ones I've encountered. She doesn't ask me what the novel's about. She knows. I frown in concentration, relieved that I don't have to worry about how I look. I speak quickly and clearly (the voice is not shaky, hooray). I don't complete any of my sentences, but am told later by my non-partisan friends that I sounded poised, even writerly.

I make Katherine laugh by referring to an appearance on her radio show as the pinnacle of success.

When it's over, I thank everyone, say goodbye, get into my car, and scream.

—

5:55 P.M.
Part of the Harbourfront Reading Series routine is dinner beforehand at a nearby restaurant. I arrive first. Joining me will be Greg Gatenby, the reading series director, and Lydia Millet, my fellow reader.

I have developed an unhealthy interest in Lydia since I found out she was to be my reading partner. I have quizzed the Harbourfront publicist about Lydia's media appearances in a tone that can only be described as competitive. I have read a description of her novel — it sounds like the kind of book I hate. My predisposition toward her is not helped by the facts that she is: a) young (28), and b) American.

She walks into the restaurant fifteen minutes late. She is tall and thin and pale, and looks nothing like her author photo. She drinks three glasses of wine and eats only salad. She mentions she went looking for both our books in several bookstores during the day and could find no copies of either. She asks if we can move out to the patio so she can smoke, and proceeds to chain when we do. She lets drop that she is currently writing her fourth (!) novel and that her second is making the rounds of publishers. Without asking, she takes and eats a piece of asparagus off Greg's plate.

I quiz her mercilessly. How big was her US print run? How was the Canadian publishing deal arranged? Who is her agent? Where does she live in Manhattan? What is her day job? (Aaagh: she writes TV scripts.)

When not conducting the interrogation, I eat a large quantity of salmon with mashed potatoes, drink water, and feel fluttery in the stomach region, a condition that will soon evolve into another case of thimble bladder.

Greg, meanwhile, drinks two pint bottles of soda water, predicts that our reading audience will probably number no more than fifty, given our collective unknown status, and tells me I'm crazy not to have an agent.

—

7:57 P.M.

Three minutes to show time. We walk over to the building where the reading will take place. Lydia will be on first. The fluttery feeling in my stomach has turned into an internal whirlpool, complete with the sound of rushing water in my ears, but Lydia is the picture of calm. To distract myself, I ask Greg how he thinks a certain novel, recently released with a big publicity push, will do.

"Your book will probably outsell that one," he says. "After all, that author is not ethnic, lesbian, or a crack addict, so what chance does she have?"

As I am neither lesbian nor a crack addict, I am a little put out by this. I smile gamely anyway. Like I've been doing all day.

We are shown to a minuscule green room and given brief instructions about timing and procedure. Lydia continues to act as if she will not be reading in thirty seconds — she applies her lipstick with a slow hand, takes forever to pull her book from her bag. I ask her whether she will use a podium or stool onstage, a choice I had deliberated at length and with much anxiety.

"Oh, I don't know," she says, "whatever."

I am instructed to sit at the front of the room for Lydia's half of the program. I scan the crowd, and try to count heads — surely there are more than fifty? (There were eighty people present, all of whom paid money to be there.)

Lydia starts off with a longish speech, reading from typewritten notes. The speech is not only clever, well-written, and erudite, but gives her book a more intellectual context than I could ever dream up for mine.

I sink into my seat. I've prepared no opening remarks, planning to start with a one-and-a-half-minute set-up that introduces the characters and nothing more.

Lydia's novel is about, among other things, survivalists, lepidoptera (moths), and cannibalism. She begins her reading with a rather dense passage that contains many Latin names for moths, but she elicits some chuckles when she switches to a bit where live hamsters are strapped to L'Eggs pantyhose containers and launched as defence artillery. I'm not kidding.

Intermission. I roam around, chat with relatives and friends, make two more visits to the bathroom.

We resume. I walk up to the podium after Greg's introduction, stunned by the quiet. An eerie calm descends on me. I speak, and am both thrilled and relieved that my voice sounds steady and sure. But I'm glad the chapter I've chosen contains some jokey lines. I need to hear noise.

I get my first laugh in the second scene, set at an office party, when the narrator says, "... then she jerked off his tie." I read on, and hear a few more peals of laughter. I start to enjoy myself. I step up the pace, give the read a little spin, attempt some comic timing. I have been a little apprehensive about reading a meant-to-be-funny part, in which the heroine's underwear becomes first wet (when lust overcomes her), then dry and crusty. But I revel in reading the lines, and am gratified by the startled female laughs of recognition that burst forth from the audience.

I end with the phrase, "... I was incapable of anything resembling rational thought," and I say, "I'm in about the same state myself right now, so thank you."

I walk off the stage and sit down amidst the applause, face flushed.

Lydia leans over and says, "Good reading!" and I feel terrible for not having told her the same.

At the autograph table, I sign twenty books, some of them for strangers. An old teenage friend, who has become a foreign affairs columnist for a major newspaper, has responded to my invitation to the reading, much to my surprise, and has brought his mother. Each of them clutches a book. I write something banal in his copy — only later do I think of the perfect inscription — and ask if he can use his influence to get the book reviewed in his newspaper. He stammers that he will try, and I am forever shamed that I asked.

—

9:30 P.M.
I get into my car and scream.

Theatrics

AS A WRITER you never know how a project is going to start, and when and where it's going to end. In the midst of writing a collection of short stories, I decided to supplement my income by working for my sister, the artistic director of a small theatre company. One day, while I was alone in the office, a woman popped her head around the door. She was from the women's health collective down the hall, and she thought it was time someone wrote a play about female body image directed at teenage girls. I looked around; there was no one else in the room. It was a fabulous idea, and even though I'd never written a play, I decided I should write this one.

At around the same time, I heard a theory that a woman should do with her life whatever she enjoyed most as a girl at the age of ten. At that age, I was writing and producing plays with my sister in our dark attic on the outskirts of London, England, complete with typewritten programs, bare light bulbs for ambiance, and a red blanket hung from a beam for a curtain. The stage was set, so to speak.

My sister said that once the play was written, she would consider producing it. But the instant she and I agreed to work together creatively, we both became terribly insecure. I made the mistake of showing her the first draft of my play as soon as it was written. She had plenty to say: it was laced with complicated ideas and didn't have enough plot or characterization; there were too many characters and she could never find that many male actors;

the set was too complex; and there were too many scene changes. "It's your first play," she said. "It's bound to need a lot of work to bring it to the stage." I countered with the tempestuousness I thought becoming to a playwright, that I was not going to change anything for purely practical considerations.

In the end, I reworked the play so that the characters could be double-cast, and cut my set requirements, but insisted that she find two male actors. One day she phoned me to inform me that there was no conflict. Without conflict, there was no story. I was devastated again. Because it was my first play, but her zillionth, I didn't realize that all this back and forthing was a normal part of the development of workshopping a play.

Then she turned her attention to the title, "Down the Rabbit Hole." Who would feel compelled to see it? What did it mean? And what on earth did it have to do with female body image? I tried to explain that Alice's journey through Wonderland embodied the frightening flight through adolescence for young girls, and that ... My sister said that it didn't matter what the reasons were, it was a bad title. So after much discussion between my mother, sister, and I, my mother came up with "Heavenly Bodies." My sister and I looked at each other: the perfect title.

Next came the read-through. I was so excited, I couldn't mingle with the actors before the read, and then the play got jammed in the photocopier, so there weren't enough copies to go around. One of the men didn't show up. We started the read without him, and finally the assistant director called him, and he was asleep. He said he couldn't commit to the part. This fulfilled my sister's prophecy: we'd lost a man *before* the initial read-through.

When they began to read the play, I was astounded. There seemed to be a plot, conflict was occurring. Things that weren't intended to be funny were transformed into hilarious one-liners. They laughed, took it seriously, and tried their best. I was floored. I was numb. It had come to life — for them. To me, as I listened, the whole thing still sounded as flat and clichéd as a dull lecture. Were they merely being polite by laughing because, I, the playwright, was there?

By the first rehearsal, a man had been found. I was so nervous that I laughed uncontrollably not only at the humour, but at all the serious parts, as well as my sister's directing cues and blocking ideas. In hindsight, my hysteria must have been relief that the play was working, that the actors and my sister were bringing to life what was rather formal dialogue.

My sister spent many extra hours meeting with costume and lighting designers. Technical decisions were made: the play would be set in thrust formation; the set and costumes would be pink. There would be hearts and diamonds from playing cards on the furniture, catching the essence of the Alice motif, though the set designer was from Quebec and had never heard of *Alice in Wonderland*.

Later on, as I watched each rehearsal, I couldn't believe that the entire thing had grown in fits and starts out of my mind and was being played out whole in front of me. There was this nagging sense that I wasn't responsible for it, that I hadn't known how it would all turn out. And if a line had to go, or a scene needed to be changed around, because we were sisters, my sister just yelled "Cut" heartlessly and the lines would be gone. I was horrified when I realized that it was my personality that was out there, paraded in the guise of a play for all to see.

As the play was blocked, and the actors began to be off-book, I attended the rehearsals to see how the play flowed. My sister and the assistant director pictured the second act as a kind of mocking dreamscape, and decided it should be acted with masks. Pink masks. And that the pink foam cake would be cut with a plastic sword.

As opening night loomed, we feared no one would come to an unknown play by an unknown writer in a small theatre. The publicist was working hard and set up publicity interviews on radio, with newspapers, and on local television. The night before my first interview, I didn't sleep. I panicked and wanted my mother. I was terrified of my own terror, because I didn't know what I was afraid of. I repeated to myself that it was a small play in a small theatre, and it didn't matter if no one came. But it was *my first play*. Then, even more terrifying, when I had the media attention, I loved it, suddenly feeling at ease in the spotlight. I turned into a media darling, calling the theatre offices to find out when my next interview was going to be, and making helpful suggestions that they could try so-and-so at such-and-such paper.

At the dress rehearsal, I fell in love. With the actors, the crew, my sister, the assistant director, life, the costume designer, the stage manager. I thought the play was the most beautiful thing ever made. I returned to laughing hysterically at my own jokes, and marvelling at the dedication of all the people working for hardly any credit and mostly for free.

On opening night, I was more hyper than I've ever been. People around me said I looked different. Glowing. The crowd was large, the lights went down, the music began, and I was still not sure who had written the thing, or if it made any sense.

That night, the crowd did respond to the work, the funny parts for sure, and I thought as I stared maniacally at them through the darkness that I saw some people cry. I discovered that silence isn't boredom, but attention, and shifting and shuffling means you've lost them. I was exposed, and it was exciting. In playwriting, as opposed to writing books, you feel the reaction, you see it happening, as each line is spoken. This is a great and terrible thing. And you do it as a team; you feel the highs and lows together. And at least there was someone else to blame if it all went wrong.

On closing night, I felt great grief that the play would never be put on in those exact circumstances, with that cast, and my sister directing, ever again.

The play was never reviewed, so I didn't go through any mind-numbing fear of what the critics would say. But we did have a comment box. We were not allowed to read the comments until the end of the run, for fear that the actors would be put off by the contents. After the last show, we opened it and read them. All but one was positive. I discovered that praise and criticism have to become equally meaningless to a creator. You don't believe the praise, and you don't want to believe the criticism, unless you thought of it already yourself, which you did when you agonized over each word time and time again.

Ironically, the play didn't die with closing night. A one-act version with the same cast toured high schools and junior highs in Calgary for almost a year. It was then used as an educational tool for young women actors, and performed at Belvoir Terrace Performing Arts school in Massachusetts, USA, a place I hadn't even known existed. I never got the name of the woman who first suggested the idea, peeping around our office door, but I wish I had. I think she should be given credit for a very good idea for a play.

Obscurity
to Obscurité in Twenty-Nine Steps

1. **PUBLISHING A FIRST BOOK** is like being drunk at a roulette wheel for three years. It requires luck, giddy naïveté, and patience. Here is the problem: no one is sure that I've actually written a book. At this early stage, this thing in my hands is barely a manuscript. Most people insist on calling it a "ms." "Ms." is an abbreviation for a woman of uncertain marital status, or a batch of papers of questionable value.

2. So, in 1992, I send her out into the street. To begin with, I'm young. I think contacts aren't necessary. Writer friends needn't help. Blurbs don't matter. I believe in the nobility of casting a novel into a publisher's slush pile. It's January, a bit cold out, so I wrap up the Ms. (I'm a polite Canadian, so I enclose a self-addressed envelope.) Then I go off to the nearest post office.

3. When I think back to this step I imagine: A clear day. My leg swinging out. A crisp pair of ironed pants with crease and a cuff. My white socks sparkle as each pant leg pulls away from my heel. It's like the first day of school. The clerk asks me how I want to send my package. I decide to

send it modestly, by standard parcel post. You don't want to appear too eager. Then she asks me to declare the value. I think about the three years of research and writing, the cost of paper and the computer, the lost wages, the beer, and all those sticky notes. I think about the museum fees, the photographs of the miners, the tape recordings, and the copying charges. I imagine some new acquisitions for the road ahead: a lottery ticket, a bottle of wine, and a funnel. Finally, I settle on the random figure of 15,432 dollars and eleven cents.

4. I have no idea (of course) that any package over five hundred dollars is always sent by armed guard. I find this out later. The publisher is required to sign for my novel at gunpoint. Not a bad thing, really. I'm certain she reads my manuscript that morning, in one sitting, no lunch, holding all her calls.

5. This strategy works so well
   I won't mail a haiku
   without one or two armed guards.

6. A month later, I receive a reader's report and the publisher's standard, hmmm-this-is-good-stuff-but-not-quite-right-for-us letter. So I revise the book, send out thirty copies, and leave for Japan the next day. I teach English in Japan for a year and a half, and wait out the rejections. In the afternoons, I coach kendo in various junior high schools. This is a sport where your opponent is dressed in black robes and he wears a spaghetti strainer on his face. A thin handkerchief and a piece of leather is all that protects the top of your head. Basically, he tries to whack the bejesus out of you with a long, bamboo stick. The perfect training for a writer. You wait for an attack, you wait and wait, and then, when you finally get some criticism, your muscles tense. In preparation for the blow, your skin thickens. You move, you parry, you block, and then you run away.

7. Yes, I left the country rather than wait out the rejections. But this stage is surprisingly painless. There are seven publishers who accept the book, including one zealous editor who offers to hack it down to a shipyard ditty. See step number eight for a fair synopsis of his editorial prowess.

8. Drowning in Darkness
   Gee, it sure is dark down here.
   Ow! That was my knee.

9. Penguin is interested, but eventually passes. Another major publisher considers my Ms. for so long that it seems to be lost in the slush pile, floating from one desk to another. On a drunken whim, I call them up and an editor (who no longer works in publishing) writes back. He says that the book is being seriously considered and that someone at the top (someone with his name) is going to look at it in the next couple of months. He ends this note with the words, "If another publisher has expressed an interest … I wouldn't hesitate to entertain their blandishments."

10. So I do. I happen to love blandishments. Sometimes I serve chips, dip, beer, and blandishments, and I entertain all night long.

11. I phone a few writer friends for advice on contracts. Aritha van Herk is supportive and offers me a blurb. Rudy Wiebe spends an hour with me, going over several contracts line by line. Despite all this advice, I still manage to misspell the word "copyright" in all my correspondence.

12. One digression: I have this idea (later on, when it's too late), that I should let these seven publishers fight over me, just a little. That's me there, the blushing bride, in lace. I'm standing near a tree. It's summer. And these manly publishers are going to fight for my honour. I flutter my eyes. They draw swords, then guns. "Over me?" I ask, feigning surprise, because I must feign something. (Nothing comes of this idea.)

13. Finally, in late September, I accept an offer because it seems important to sign the thing before I turn twenty-eight. The publisher, a woman named Jan Geddes, phones me immediately.

14. About Jan: She's a generous reader and becomes a great friend. I tell her I want to make some changes, add two folktales and the sound of birds, etc. Her editorial advice is: "Don't change too much." She believes in the book as I'd envisioned it. What's more, she's had some early success with another Italian-Canadian writer named Nino. And in the end, that's all you really need, a publisher who'll be a good match for you, one who believes in the book and promotes it every waking hour of the day.

15. In Japan, the book business is so difficult to crack that publishers host one literary competition per year for unknown writers. It would be like Knopf hosting the only fantasy competition in the country and

Penguin agreeing to host the children's competition, etc. Everything is orchestrated from the top. It's as civil as going to med school. Here's how it works: you can enter only one competition. If you don't get published, you are honour-bound to go away and write another book. If you win a competition, only then can you go back and have your first efforts published. The Japanese regard this editorial competition as fair play, and they limit the number of new books flooding their market. Established authors don't seem to mind because they retain a greater percentage of profits. If you can break into the Japanese market, it's possible to retire on your first novel royalties.

16. In Japan, a literary controversy develops only when a writer wins a "kiddy litter" competition with an adult novel. This strikes them as unfair, but it happens routinely.

17. Back to me. December hits. The weather turns cold and damp. My leather shoes are green with mould, yet it's difficult not to grin like an idiot for the author photo. I spend my days travelling to different schools on the Kanto Plain surrounding Tokyo dressed as Santa Claus. I spend my nights fiddling with the missus.

18. Flush with Christmas cheer and impending publication, I write about a murder I'd witnessed in Vancouver. I send the piece off to a certain Canadian magazine. They write back that they already have someone working on the story. This comes as some surprise because I'd told only one person about it. (Let's call him The Big Luanda.) I make an inquiry. "Yes, yes, it's the same fellow, it's The Big Luanda, and we've got him." The next day, I receive a threatening fax from the magazine's legal department, which I ignore. Luanda calls, begs forgiveness, then asks for my notes. Inexplicably, I send them. This is called "paying my dues," I think. Something good will come of this, I decide. A writing credit, perhaps. (Not!) Good Karma? (Plenty of it.) Four months later, after an editorial change, the magazine abandons their article and pays The Big Luanda a "kill fee." I publish my own version in *Brick*. From this morality tale, I learn two things: You can hang a happy ending on a murder story and Big Luandas are the same as Little Luandas.

19. I come back to Canada in May and meet Jan at a Toronto book fair. Someone points her out to me and I look across the show floor to see a tall, elegant woman in a green blouse. Her hair is long and brown. She

is on her way back from lunch and she has sauerkraut and mustard in her hair. "Oh!" she says. "I can't imagine what you must think of me! Your publisher has a hot dog in her hair!" Her voice is reedy but enthusiastic. "Well," I say, "this is uncanny. I was hoping for a publisher with a hot dog in her hair."

20. The two greatest moments in publishing a book: 1) cleaning all the notes, stickies, revisions, scraps of memoranda, and photos off your desk; and 2) receiving the first copy of your published novel in the mail. I open the box and slap a bound copy into my father's hand with a satisfying "wrop."

21. *Drowning in Darkness* is launched in September, one year after I sign with Cormorant. This is what happens: Jan quickly sells the Spanish rights to a publisher in Barcelona. Then she licenses the remainder to an in-house Canadian agent. Let's call him Biff. Now, Biff has a complicated algorithm for surviving life's rocky patches. He doesn't get out of bed unless he receives a percentage of European book sales that cost more than a pair of Louis Vuitton suspenders. You see, Biff doesn't eat breakfast. Biff is a Master of the Long Lunch — this is his trade, his specialization, his genre. A long lunch = a good contact. A good contact "speaks volumes." Biff is hard to reach because he's regularly speaking volumes, over lunch, and this makes him appear more valuable to the rest of us who are hunting him down for answers. Despite the good reviews in Canada and Spain, my book is an inheritance for him, a bastard child that he can't seem to read. To his surprise, a movie director voices interest in the book. I send Biff a film synopsis to help him along. Then I ask him for the reviews from Spain (which never appear). I ask him for the financials (which never appear). "I'll look into that," he says. Sometimes I call to say, Hello Biff! How's everything? Biff stops returning my calls. I imagine Biff lunching with important people and snapping his marvellous suspenders.

22. Have you heard about this racket? The Canadian book tour is a drunken wonderland. I'm given a fistful of plane tickets, and then I'm set loose across the country. Publicity assistants wait for my arrival holding my name over their breasts. I tour country music stations and lunch with print journalists. The CBC studios are dimly lit, with brown windows. It's like walking through a bran muffin.

23. One radio jockey asks me about Italian superstitions, question after question, which I fend off in general terms. He pries further. There's something more here isn't there? *Yes*, I say. He's an investigative journalist, so he probes for answers. He hasn't read the book, but he wants to know about these superstitions; he wants to know how the Calabrese women of Bagnara shed misfortune. I'm keeping him away from the truth because I'm not sure if this sort of material is appropriate for live (province-wide) radio at 4 P.M. on a Tuesday. But his forehead dips toward the table, as if to focus on the interrogation. "What do they do?" he asks. "How do they do it? Eh? Eh?" "The men lie down," I say. "Hmm?" he says. "And the women of Bagnara stand over them." "Yes, yes. Go on." "And then they pee on their husbands!" His head shoots back, the earphones bounce off the padded wall, and the show ends.

24. With print journalists, I become a bit too careful with my speech. I want to be quoted accurately, but I develop a "poetic" or "thoughtful" reputation that I just can't shake. This description follows me across Canada from one newspaper to the next.

25. After each event, I'm carried to dinner and drinks. We swim through floating sushi bars and Tiki joints, Italian cafés and ginger soup kitchens. In the mornings, my eyelids are purple and rimmed with crust. My clothes smell like cigarettes and dated tuna. It's 7 A.M., so I push myself toward another airport and (on the plane) another hour of sleep.

26. On the last leg, I board the plane from Saskatoon to Calgary. I pass the requisite Grisham readers, yes, Grisham, Grisham, Grisham, Danielle Steele, Grisham, Grisham, and discover that one woman is reading my novel, just across the aisle from my chair. She thumbs my pages, she looks at the back cover and she sees my photograph, the "serious" one from Japan. She reads the blurbs, then she opens the book, my old Ms., and she begins to read. She reads, and then she turns the first page, and this all seems extraordinary to me. An airline attendant interrupts her and makes her buckle up. The plane tips and she flips to page two. I watch her eyes open slightly, something has surprised her at the top of page three, midway down. I'll have to look at that spot, I decide. I'd better check that bit. Then the attendant, a peevish fellow with hair the colour of straw, brushes between us. For an instant, I've lost my gentle reader. Then I see her and the attendant. This bottle-blonde *cretino*

hands her a newspaper and she drops my novel into her bag. She reads the business section, classified, home and garden. She reads the wrestling statistics, the obituaries, and the weather in resort locations. She reads the entire newspaper, while I try to chew open a mini bag of mixed nuts.

27. Jan sells Cormorant. Suddenly I'm dealing with someone named Boff. With the help of two lawyers and a different pair of suspenders, I contact Boff and fire Biff. Boff is miffed that Biff is boffed. This actually takes several years of artful, guilt-ridden negotiation. It's all very complicated because Boff has no records and Biff didn't keep track of his luncheon companions. They confer for months. Seasons pass and come round again. While they confer, I marry one of my lawyers. (The pretty one.) Finally, Biff and Boff send me their first official report. "There are no records," says Boff, "because the book wasn't published in Spain! But we're still here, working hard for you!" I fax Biff and Boff a copy of the Spanish edition, *Ahogado en la Oscuridad*. I fax them all 215 translated pages. This tactic works well for asserting copyright and I recommend it to everyone. Within an hour, I reacquire my world rights and pack a suitcase.

28. In Paris, I meet an editor at Gallimard Press. Her father was the gutsy man who published *Barbarella*. We talk Barthes and jazz. Her husband loves Barthes and jazz so she brings me home. Soon we're all eating oysters and soft cheese. We're drinking white wine from flutes. Lunch stretches on for miles.

29. So, here I am in 2004. I'm back in Canada, waiting for my French publication, *Parmi les ombres*. As with the (imaginary) Spanish translation, my French translator's questions revolve around mining terms and expletives. Every week or so, she calls and if I'm outside, raking the yard, she leaves a message on the machine. She has a lovely Parisian accent. She's a novelist, as well as a translator. Her name is Marie-Hélène. In her voice, I can hear the River Seine and the leaves scratching across Saint-Germain. I can hear the teacups rattling at Ladurée. Her questions resemble the latest e-mail offers from Viagra: "Excusez-moi, Peeterr, what does it mean, this prick of a wind?" I have no idea, I say. But I'll look into it.

"A Suitable Publisher,"

or Getting that First Book Published

ACTUALLY IT'S NOT MY FIRST BOOK, but that's part of the problem. I've been involved, as author, co-author, editor, or co-editor with the publication of eight books. Those, however, were all academic works. And in the rosy glow of retrospect, it seems they were a lot easier to get published than my first, single book of poems. Easier at least in the sense that the process didn't involve the receipt of rejection after rejection.

Prior to attending the Banff writing studio in the fall of 1999, I had briefly considered an offer to self-publish from within a publishing collective. I found the offer initially appealing. It made me feel accepted by at least one group of writers of poetry, and I was becoming impatient about getting a book out. But several poets talked me out of it, persuading me that I would feel better if I had the patience and perseverance to undergo the evaluation process involved in submission to an independent, literary press. I took the advice.

My belief in my own ability was strengthened by the five weeks at Banff. Indeed, the experience gave me a terrific high, as I suspect it does almost everyone who is lucky enough to take part in one of its artists' programs. In this state of semi-euphoria, I assembled the first version of a poetry manuscript and, in late December 1999, sent it out to five publishing houses.

The Banff high lasted until the arrival, in early January 2000, of the first rejection of my manuscript. What made it particularly devastating was the manner in which it came: an unsigned form letter bearing my name, the number assigned to my submission (#99095), its title, and the date received written above the typed, impersonal words. Even worse, the editor had circled in pencil a spelling error that had escaped my scrutiny. I felt like a delinquent graduate student.

No subsequent rejection has been as unnerving as that one. Fortunately, a friend counselled me to look upon the rejection as a necessary stage toward becoming a better writer. It was good advice, however difficult to swallow. I felt especially vulnerable at the time, as I had made the decision to enter early retirement, not realizing how destabilizing it would be to give up an established professional identity to become an unknown writer.

Early in February 2000, around the time of my sixty-second birthday, my spirits got a lift. A press informed me that my manuscript had made it through round one. When their final rejection arrived a few months later, I felt disappointed, but the letter let me down gently. Shortly after this communication, I heard negatively from a third press. Early in June 2000, I sent out inquiries to three additional presses.

I heard back almost immediately from one of these. The press was "full up for poetry" over its next two lists. The next news came in the middle of July, a letter requesting the complete manuscript for consideration. My hopes soared. I called one of my poetry mentors and she said this was a very promising sign. Now, she assured me, it was only a matter of time until my manuscript found its niche.

Not long afterward, I received word that I had been accepted into the new Banff Wired Writing Program. That I applied is an indication of my awareness that I could benefit from editorial help with my manuscript and with my poetry writing in general. I again met up with an impressive group of talented writers, and I was assigned to work with Ken Babstock, who proved to be an excellent editor.

Toward the end of summer, I decided that I had waited long enough to hear from two of the presses in my initial submission. A call to one of these prompted a diplomatic letter, dated August 16, stating that obligations to their previously published poets prevented them from taking my project on.

Not having been able to reach the other press by phone, I sent a letter of inquiry on September 19. On the evening of September 29, just one day before I was to fly to Banff, I logged on to my e-mail, which I hadn't bothered to read for a few days. To my astonishment, the press had sent me a message three days earlier, apologizing for the long delay in attending to my initial submission, and requesting "to see the entire manuscript." I rushed around like a mad woman (I hadn't yet finished my packing for Banff), managing to print out (and revise in places while printing) a copy of the entire manuscript that evening. The next morning, I arranged for Purolator to pick up the package at my house, where I would leave it behind the storm door before I left for the airport. On the mid-October evening I arrived back in Toronto from Banff, I walked into the house, empty except for our two cats (my partner was away on sabbatical), and spied in the mail, piled up and waiting for me, the big, fat, self-addressed envelope containing my manuscript. It was a rejection from the press for which I'd had such high hopes. My Banff-induced exhilaration evaporated. Perhaps I felt as low as I did because the news hit me when I was in a state of exhaustion from a day of travel. Along with the rejection came some severe criticism: the press's director had noted that, while he enjoyed the poems' "many fine lines and strong images," he "also found that the poems did not often enough rise above the purely personal." This was criticism that, in revising the manuscript, I took to heart.

Only three weeks later, I got word from the sole remaining press to which I had sent only a sample that they were interested in seeing the entire manuscript. I took a little over a week before sending it off, and during that time, with the help of my wired writing editor, Ken, I revised the manuscript considerably, culling weaker poems and adding new ones I had written over the summer and while at Banff. I also came up with what I thought was a more fitting title for the book: " The Scent of an Orange" gave way to "Roots, Rocks, Straws." With two presses still expressing interest, I felt all was not completely lost.

My life settled into something of a routine. I enrolled in a master's poetry class offered on Thursday evenings through the University of Toronto's continuing education program, met with my poetry group on Monday evenings, and arranged to meet with my Banff wired writing editor approximately once a week. Living not far from one another in Toronto allowed us to bypass the "wired" aspect of the program. I now spent a part of almost every day working on and reading poetry. But every day there was the agonizing wait for the mail. And for some reason, the mail in my neighbourhood began to be delivered later and later in the day, often not arriving until after 5:00 P.M. From upstairs where I was working on my computer, I could hear the muffled thud of the mail hitting the front hall floor. Day after day, I would rush down, full of expectation, only to find junk mail or bills.

Adapting to my new career, I also began applying for workshops, writing programs, and retreats outside Canada. At the end of June 2000, I attended a workshop with the North Carolina poet and novelist Fred Chappell, held in Duluth, Minnesota. In early January 2001, I flew to Mexico to participate in the poetry week held every year in the colonial town of San Miguel de Allende. Workshops with Carolyn Kizer, Stephen Dunn, and Leslie Ullman were the draw.

My arrival back in Toronto in mid-January 2001 repeated the experience of my return from Banff in mid-October 2000. Energy depleted by almost twelve hours of travel, I entered an empty house only to discover the dreaded fat envelope containing my manuscript. But this rejection praised my poetry, calling my manuscript "an accomplished and compelling collection of poems," and expressing regret at not being able to accept it for publication. The reason: "We are limited in the number of poetry books that we publish (at most, one or two each season) and we are often in this position of having to make difficult decisions." I felt I had come close.

That left one outstanding submission and the fear that it, too, would meet with rejection. I began to draw up a list in my head of possible presses for a third set of submissions, but I was dreading the start of a new round of waiting. From my experience, the process could last anywhere from seven months to over a year. I joked that I hoped my first book would come out before I had to use a walker to reach the podium.

In early March 2001, I dreamed I was standing on a sandy beach (I had just returned from visiting my partner, who was on sabbatical at the University of Hawaii), when a large, self-addressed envelope washed up at my feet. Stooping to pick it up, I thought, here it is again, another rejection, but as I slit the envelope open, I found no such letter, only written comments on the manuscript, suggestions for possible revision. It slowly dawned on me, the manuscript had been accepted, not rejected, and I was flooded with happiness. Waking, I berated myself. The folly of believing in such a dream would just make the inevitable rejection all the more difficult to overcome.

Nevertheless, late that afternoon, sitting at my computer at the end of a writing day, I decided to check my e-mail one more time. With trepidation, I clicked on the one new message and read:

Dear Ruth Roach Pierson,

I'm e-mailing you concerning your poetry manuscript. I would like to publish it, and I need to know if it is still available. If it is, and if you are still interested in BuschekBooks, then I will send you along a more detailed letter in order for you to make a final decision.

I'm looking at next spring (2002) as the publication date.

Thanks for your interest in BuschekBooks.
John Buschek

I sat there stunned. After a bit, I was able to pull myself together and respond that, yes, my manuscript was still available and I would be thrilled to be published by BuschekBooks.

And then I started calling everyone I could think of who might be interested in hearing my good news. Late in the evening, though home alone, I broke out a bottle of cheap champagne and toasted my success. By Wednesday, I was celebrating more seriously with friends (and drinking a better brand of sparkling wine). Also by Wednesday, my elation began to yield to worry (that I'd never be able to get my manuscript into good enough shape by spring 2002) and paranoid fantasies (that the e-mail message was a hoax, or a mistake and really meant for another).

My first book, *Where No Window Was*, was published in March 2002.

Is **Anybody** Out There?

EARLY ON IN MY CAREER, Daphne Marlatt, my instructor at the time, suggested that writing was about having a conversation. What we all needed was to find who we wanted to speak to and speak to them: plausible enough, but intimidating. And certainly enough work to keep me busy for the next ten years. But, after ten years, I finally found myself with a manuscript in hand — it seemed I had found my place in the conversation. Or so I thought. But now came the hard part: finding a publisher.

How exactly does one go about finding a publisher? It's a complex undertaking. Perhaps naively, I never thought much beyond writing the poem, and perhaps reading it, or sending it off to a journal. The shape of the book, the cover, acknowledgments, dedications, never mind the name of the publisher — to my astonishment, none of this had occurred to me. I mulled this over for a bit, consulted friends, and got conflicting advice: send the whole manuscript off to one publisher, send a sample off to many, tell them you're simultaneously submitting, don't mention anything. If this wasn't confusing enough, there was that other, more pressing matter — where should I send it?

"Well, who're you talking to?" I heard Daphne Marlatt asking. "Which books would you like to see your offering on the shelf next to? Who do you want to rub covers with?" Good question. Who? Who had I written these poems in conversation with? Which led me to a thorough scanning of all the poetry books I'd ever read and some I hadn't. I spent hours in bookstores, pestering friends, begging my partner to listen as I rambled off attributes of this or that press. I kept thinking that if I were a "better writer" this wouldn't be a question — that somehow I had missed an essential step in my development, that I should "just know" where my book belonged. The fact of the matter was I had no clue.

I decided I had to send the manuscript off to the presses that published the books I most respected. So I made a list of those. Then I made a list of presses I thought were edgy, that had chutzpah and might hold unexpected pleasures. (It was a short list.) After that, I added the historically significant presses. Then I went through and cut out some of the presses I respect enormously but with whom I knew my work wouldn't fit (a little too much polyester with the linen set). Once I had my final list, I wrote cover letters (in which I suggested multiple submissions and urged the publishers to contact me to see the whole manuscript), printed out a sample of the manu-script, addressed envelopes, mailed them, and tried to forget about it.

But of course I didn't forget. Instead, I turned into Woody Allen on amphetamines. "Who am I kidding," I found myself blurting out in grocery store lineups, "I can't write. How could I have had the nerve to send my manuscript there?" Once I woke up at 5 A.M. from a nightmare featuring Michael Ondaatje and Margaret Atwood toasting marshmallows over my best work. I imagined ending up in a slush pile of worst-ever submissions; I imagined a long, loud howl of laughter with the opening of every lovingly addressed manila envelope. I told myself I didn't care at all, but I moved my lawn chair to the front of the house to better observe the patterns of our postal carrier.

Suddenly, envelopes addressed with my own confident writing began drifting back into my arms, and the next phase of my so-called writing career began. Oddly enough, once the replies started coming — a healthy mixture of outright rejection, cautious curiosity, and real interest — the whole idea of what I thought was the conversation kicked in. It's an impor-tant decision, like choosing a midwife for a birth. I wanted someone skilled, of course, though in the end I wouldn't choose pure skill over bedside manner. I wanted someone confident, but not so confident that they didn't need to consult me. I wanted someone who believed in the work, but not so blindly, that it wouldn't be well edited. Ultimately, I wanted someone I could talk to.

—

December 5, 2004

My first book of poetry, *Slip,* was published weeks after 9/11. I was teaching in New Jersey. Classes were cancelled. The air was acrid. People wandered around trying to donate blood. Grades dropped. Winter never arrived. There was some talk of cancelling or putting off publication, but in the end my book bumped into the fractured world, and was handed to me moments before I had to read from it at my launch in Toronto. A few weeks later, my father passed away. Did I feel in conversation with my press? My editor? Anyone? Frankly, no. In fact, the notion of speaking seemed impossible. But then there were the audiences: a vibrant group of undergraduates in Antigonish, strangers in Seattle, friends in Vancouver, a room full of eclectic young writers in Victoria — reading the poems allowed for a point of connection, a release even, and this was essential, especially post 9/11. In the context of reading, what I had to say suddenly seemed relevant.

Now that I have published my second book, I realize there are all kinds of conversations going on. And while publication is nice, the page or the stage is where the conversations are going on that really excite me. On the page, I'm in direct dialogue with the writers who inspire me; on the stage, I'm a conduit for the energy that is poetry — not just me, or my words, but the whole grand connective muscle that is poetry. Yes, by publishing a book you enter the conversation, but the book after all is the shell: it's still the act of writing that offers the greatest pleasure to the author, and the act of reading that allows you to speak directly to people. Just as it's not necessarily the book, or even the act of reading, but the inspiration, release, or joy that comes from hearing or reading poetry, that keeps the reader scrambling for that next great book.

GLORIA SAWAI

When They Won't Leave

On the Process of Writing
A Song for Nettie Johnson

MANY YEARS AGO, in my teens, I wrote a poem about a man sitting in a dusty cellar praying, and a girl (me, I guess) crouched on the stair's landing looking down on him. The cellar smelled of coal dust. I don't remember this event actually happening. True, the basements in our Saskatchewan homes were dark and dusty, and my dad, a preacher, sometimes prayed out loud — in his study or at the kitchen table. Not, to my knowledge, in the basement. Nothing came of the poem. It was lost or discarded with other scraps of my childhood.

Much later, as an adult, I enrolled in a playwriting course. I chose as the setting for my play a dusty basement, with two men sitting in front of the furnace — a preacher and a musician. (Was the musician Emil Barstad, who directed the church choir in Preeceville, Saskatchewan, and who could get the choir to sing the "Hallelujah Chorus"? Or was it the choir director I'd heard about, in another town, a man with a drinking problem, who was sober just often enough to keep his job?) Three children crouched on the landing, watching. But this play, like the poem, went nowhere.

Since I needed to fulfill the course assignment, I began a new play. The setting was a stone quarry on the Saskatchewan prairie. A woman sat in a rocking chair beside the gravel pit and spelled aloud. I don't know where this woman came from, why she lived at the quarry, why she stared into the pit, or why she spelled. (Although I do remember a speller I had in grade two and the first three words on one of the lists: ball, school, girl.) I got a bit further in this play. Children from the town came out to the quarry and harassed the woman, calling her names and throwing stones. (As my friends and I had done to Mrs. Lazoon? Throwing stones against her house and at her chickens, waiting for her to come out and yell at us?) This play, too, didn't go anywhere and I abandoned it. What I finally wrote for the course was a play about a massive and deadly atomic bomb attack that destroyed most of the earth. I handed the assignment in, late and incomplete. I failed the course.

That was the end of playwriting for me until a year or two later when the idea suddenly occurred to me that the three characters — the musician, the woman, and the preacher — all belonged in the same play. So I began again. I moved the musician, Eli, out to the quarry to live in a trailer with Nettie, the woman who spelled. And I had Eli sojourn into town to meet the preacher in his basement in front of the furnace, where he would try to convince the preacher to let him direct the church choir. I found this set-up interesting and compelling. Now the story had somewhere to go. I completed the play, called it *Saskatchewan Hallelujah*, sent it to various theatres, and was rejected by all of them. So I turned my attention to the short story form, which I'd had some success with, in that my stories were usually published.

But for some reason, Eli and Nettie would not leave me in peace. I enrolled in a television screenwriting course and chose the same characters, same setting, same story for my script. I learned that the stronger the obsessions of the characters, the more chance there is for conflict and energy. I enjoyed the course and finished the play, but I had little confidence in my dramatic abilities and didn't bother to send the script out.

By this time I was fed up with Eli, Nettie, and the whole Saskatchewan prairie and hoped they'd disappear. But, no. A few years later, I settled into a studio in The Banff Centre's Leighton Colony, determined to get a lot of work done. Adele Wiseman was the director of the writing program at the time. The thought struck me that the stage play, *Saskatchewan Hallelujah*, would actually make a good story, a long short story, or maybe even a novella. I thought, too, that Eli and Nettie deserved to come out of the bottom drawer and finally be recognized. So I began work on a long story, which I eventually called "A Song for Nettie Johnson." Changing a play into a story wasn't easy for me. It took a long time. One night at the supper table in the centre's dining room, Adele asked me, "How did the writing go today?" I said, "Good. I got Eli up the hill." (This event occurs in the beginning of the story where Eli is on his way into town to see the preacher.) Adele said, "Yes, it's important to get up the hill." And we had a pleasant supper to celebrate the occasion.

I finished the story during another stint at the Leighton Colony some time later. The writing experience this time was much more enjoyable. I was able to check out books and tapes from the centre's library, and listen to Handel's *Messiah* as I followed the score. I plotted how many songs could be sung during Nettie's trek into town. I loved sitting in the studio, looking out at the snow-laden pine trees (I think it was winter, but maybe I just wish it was), and listening to "Comfort ye my People. Speak comfortably to Jerusalem, and cry unto her that her warfare is accomplished ..."

Then, in 1998, I was a participant in the May studio, again at The Banff Centre. Edna Alford was my mentor. I brought with me all the stories I'd written, planning to revise and polish them with the hope that they could form a collection for publication. I focused particularly on the novella, "A Song for Nettie Johnson." Edna was a marvellous editor for me. She'd say things like, "The prairie should be more beautiful." And I'd insert a purple vetch beside a rock. Or referring to the story, "Memorial," she'd say, "I think there needs to be more yellow here." And I'd change the grey face of the corpse to a yellowish grey.

This part of the writing process was almost pure pleasure for me because the hard work of creation had already been done, and now I was just fixing things up here and there. Edna also helped arrange the stories into a suitable sequence. Now the collection was complete, except for one story, which I wrote after I left Banff — "Oh Wild Flock, Oh Crimson Sky." This became my favourite story, perhaps because I enjoyed all the characters in it, especially the Haugean grandfather, who was drawn from my own grandfather. (Of course, all the events in the story are fictitious.) Writing this was a pleasure, and the story was completed in a matter of a few months.

I don't understand the process of writing fiction — why one story takes twenty-five years to write, another a few months, and yet another (like "Mother's Day") a few days. Nor do I understand where the idea for a story comes from, where the seed of it, lodged in the brain, originates, or how long the seed can lie dormant before its thin shell splits open and a fragment of memory shoots up — a memory of something seen, or read or heard about, or felt or smelled, something often so simple, why even give it a second thought. But there it is, waiting for the imagination to be let loose on it, to give it growth and shape, and even touches of beauty.

Thanks to Coteau Books in Regina, *A Song for Nettie Johnson* was finally published; and the book became a success, receiving a few prizes, including the Governor General's Literary Award for Fiction in 2002. Nettie and Eli are no longer harassing me. I'm working on a new story set on an island far from Saskatchewan, and peopled with new characters. Right now, I'm finding these characters tiresome and would rather not spend time with them. But they won't leave.

BARBARA SCOTT

Through the Clouds

WHEN I WAS TWELVE, I came upon a room that held all the enchantment of C. S. Lewis's wardrobe, a gateway to Narnia and all other magical worlds besides. It was a small, second-storey room, lined floor to ceiling with bookshelves. An old oak desk stood in one corner, a battered leather couch in the other. Ivy struggled to climb in at the window sill, and even when the scents of an English spring drifted through the open window, the musty, addictive smell of books in slow decay hung throughout the room. This was my Great-Uncle Leslie's library. I spent almost the entire month of vacation (when my parents weren't dragging me off to tourist sights and family dinners) exploring the shelves, discovering in the process a novel by one of Uncle Leslie's friends, whom I was allowed to address as Uncle Stan. I couldn't believe my luck. Not only had I found paradise in the form of a private library, I had met an actual *live* author.

I wasn't all that impressed with Uncle Stan's book, which was a dated knock-off of the Jeeves adventures so popular in the 1930s; nonetheless, I hunted through the shelves for his second effort. There wasn't one. There were numerous hardcover relics by all manner of other writers I had never heard of, but nothing further by Uncle Stan. A voracious reader, I had already consumed every Nancy Drew mystery, every novel and story that Louisa May Alcott and Lucy Maud Montgomery had ever produced; I had memorized the Narnia series, and I was just starting to devour works by those prolific writers, Georgette Heyer, Agatha Christie, and Jean Plaidy. Back then, I assumed the duty of an author was to produce volume after volume for delighted fans until death did them part. Why had Uncle Stan written only one?

He wasn't the only author to betray me in such a way: Margaret Mitchell and Harper Lee also let me down. Maybe Uncle Stan had written another book and just couldn't find another publisher, but what of these two who left the field in full glory? Once inducted into the magic company of authors, why would anyone wish to leave? It was a mystery I left unexplored for more than twenty years.

I am returning to it now because in 1999 I published my first book, and the question of how, and especially why, to write the second has been consuming much of what could be actual writing time. So I've come to look again at these "one-book wonders" through the filter of my own experience.

I should clarify that my hesitation over my second book is not based on any bad experiences with my first. The moment I was told it would be published I felt pure joy. None of the petty and not-so-petty irrritants life threw at me could wipe the grin off my face for six months. My publisher and editor, even the publicist, might not have loved (in the sense of yearning over) my book more than I did (no one could), but they believed in it more. Of course, I might have fallen in love (for I did) with anyone who had agreed to bring out my book, rather in the way we're told a duckling will imprint on whatever object its eyes first light on when it emerges, sticky and dazed, from the shell. But if this is so, then I was doubly lucky in finding a publisher who would say, as Jan Geddes did when I delayed the schedule by requesting more time for edits only I thought necessary, "The most important thing is that you're happy with the book." And I was; I am. Even so, I hesitate before entering the arena again.

There are always excellent reasons not to write a book: for one thing, it's such bloody hard work; for another, there are so many books already out there, and thousands more arriving every year, ranging from the superb to the simply awful — why should yours swell their number? Publishing that first book is like reaching the first leaf on Jack's beanstalk: it takes all your efforts to clamber up there, and only when you're catching your breath do you see that the vines stretch up past the clouds. Where will you find the energy for the rest of the climb? I managed the first book almost on a dare: Can I fill that many pages? Can I find a publisher? Will anyone read it, like it? Once the "can I?" questions have been answered, you move on to the "why should I?" ones, and they're tougher to puzzle out.

But I found another question even more disturbing. Ashamed as I am to admit it, and in spite of how happy I was during the actual work on the book, after it came out I found myself asking, "Is this all?" The collection did well, by which I mean that it was favourably reviewed in a number of papers and magazines, was launched at the Eden Mills Festival, won a couple of awards. All of my friends assumed I must be over the moon, or at least able to get a great view of it from what felt to me like my most precarious position on the beanstalk. But even these rewards, delightful at the time, still left the nagging question — is that all?

While I hadn't been naive enough to think that publishing would bring me fame or fortune, I think I was secretly hoping for induction into that special club of "authors": I would feel I had "arrived," changed in some ineffable but unmistakable way. Instead, during the year of the first book, I came the closest I ever have to believing that I do, in fact, live the barren, book-bound, repressed life of the intellectual that is the cultural stereotype of the childless, later-in-life writer like me. Instead of answering questions and settling uncertainties, publication opened up a minefield of new insecurities, new existential quandaries. A hundred and fifty pages didn't seem like much to hold up as the repository for all my sacrifices of time, income, even relationships. Because the other thing I discovered about publishing a book is that, once it finally hits the shelves, you can barely stand it any more. You have reached that stage of intimacy where all you can see is the warts and nose hair and you want out. Yet, this is also the point at which you need to find the guts to tackle the next book. To discover whether you even want to, and if so — why?

Part of the difficulty with moving on to the next project, I think, is that once it leaves your hands, the first book solidifies behind you, petrifies into something you bounce up against at readings, something you don't always believe you wrote. All the carving is completed, the lucky missteps masquerading as deliberate, interpreted by reviewers and other readers as part of the design. It's seductive to believe the sham, to forget the tentative steps taken in the beginning, the huge act of faith required to open the computer file. You can't even remember where the ideas came from — there they are, with the smug remoteness of stone, offering no hint of how to tackle the next project. Surely you don't have to begin in the mud again, dabbling and throwing it about like a primate? Surely there must be some dignity to the process this time, not that desperate mulching and grubbing that somehow stirred a few slender seeds to twisting life? Weren't you supposed to learn something that would save you all this?

This reluctance to get my hands dirty reveals another, almost embarrassing, fact: in a way, I solidified too. I felt it calcifying around me, the persona of "the writer." A number of people were indeed treating me as if I had "arrived," which was fun for a while, but to my dismay I accumulated none of the inner conviction I had expected. I wanted the changes to be internal, and instead they were external, and happening to a persona which seemed, with every review and interview, to be layered upon me like a plaster cast. "Compassionate," I was called, someone "who has thought deeply," which is all very nice, but it's strange and unsettling to see yourself from the outside, even if, perhaps especially if, the view is flattering. Inside the shell, I was as confused as ever, possibly more so, as the distance yawned between the person being constructed by reviewers and publicists, and the one who had to forget about "thinking deeply" and get down to the grubby business of writing. There seemed no way to reconcile the two. I had poured everything I had into the book; I was hollowed out. If someone had thought to rap a knuckle on my chest I would have echoed. For a while it felt as though the hollowness would be permanent.

Then one day I sat down with Flannery O'Connor's essays. I sucked them up, put off all I was supposed to be doing. I wasn't writing, had accepted that. Perhaps I was tired, perhaps drained, perhaps lazy. But as I read those essays, her wry, spare voice reconnected me to what is the most important part, for me, of the writing endeavour — the sense that I am linked with a community that transcends region, time, space, body. I spent the afternoon copying phrases into a computer file of favourite passages — smiling, absorbing her tone through my fingers. I didn't care any more what my work or my life might look like to critics or reviewers, to family or friends. The thrumming of language and the percussion of computer keys resonated through me. The husk fell away.

My loft is lined almost floor to ceiling with double-stacked bookshelves, and to get to my desk, I have to negotiate a maze of books scattered over the floor. Stuffed in one corner is a cheap Ikea chair instead of a battered leather sofa, and at my window a sturdy jack pine chattering with magpies and squirrels stands in place of crowding vines and an English spring. But my room has the spirit of the library I discovered all those years ago, my gateway to other worlds, created out of the materials I had to hand. It is a sanctuary, and to sit here, with a book in front of me, computer humming, coffee cooling unnoticed — all this fills me with joy and gratitude. All this fills.

Then one day, a friend phones and says, Would you write an essay on the experience of publishing a first book? And I, knowing that I haven't written a stroke in months, foolishly say yes.

So now, in the aftermath of the first book, and thanks to my family of writers both living and dead, I'm beginning to rediscover my writing practice, to discover that I do indeed have one. This slipping and sliding through the sticky mud of memory, this messy grubbing — this is it. I'm beginning to recall that the first book started the same way, with scratching and sniffing at buried things to see if they're alive. I'm beginning to realize that writing a book, whether first or second or tenth, is not like getting to the first leaf on the stalk at all. You start each time at ground level, with poking into the earth a dried husk that doesn't look all that promising, watering anxiously, while resisting the urge to pull up the meagre sprouts to see how they're doing. Suddenly you're looking up at a monstrous growth that isn't remotely like what you thought you'd planted and that you have to chop back with nail clippers; you're clambering up into the ogre's lair and, if you're lucky, escaping with not only your life, but a few golden eggs. After you scramble down the stalk, you hack it back to the root, and let it stiffen into death. In time, you'll look down at the twisted arrangement of dried stalks with affection, but also with detachment, pick up a few dried seeds, and put them in your pocket. When you have rested, when you've had time to catch your breath, your courage, your will, maybe you'll plant them and start the whole process all over again. For some, like my Uncle Stan, the one attempt was enough; the "can I?" questions answered, perhaps he was content to tell the story of his one great adventure by a fireside to whomever would listen.

I am tempted to do the same. Now that I've attained some distance from it, I like my book again, and the life it opened up for me, for it did change things. But even as I feel the pull of the armchair, I'm stirring the dirt with one toe, and rattling the seeds in my palm. It helps to remind myself that

Jack wasn't brave, or wise, just a fool who traded bovine security for headier climes, and did so more than once. The official version is that he went looking for treasure, but I'd bet every golden egg I could muster that he simply couldn't resist the lure of that moment long before there was any hint of reward, when he poked his head through the clouds, a goofy grin on his face, and looked around to see what kind of mess he could get himself into this time.

ANNE SIMPSON

Flying into the Wild Blue Yonder

Revising a First Novel

AFTER THE CONTRACT for the first book has been signed, after interviews have been practised close to the bathroom mirror in that stage whisper only the bathroom mirror knows — only then, maybe while you're lying awake in the middle of the night, do you realize, abruptly, that you actually have to hunker down and revise your manuscript. Your editor has already begun to nudge you in this direction, perhaps soothingly, perhaps firmly. You get up from bed, pace back and forth from bedroom to kitchen, and think about how the revisions can be done, can't be done, *can* be done.

Revisions, if they are to be good ones, often depend on a good editor. Some editors go through the manuscript with a fine-toothed comb. Others stand back from a writer's manuscript and give global advice; this can work surprisingly well, but it's still hard to figure out how to solve problems.

My first novel was accepted by Penguin Canada in March 2000, with a publication date of spring 2001. This gave me lots of time to work on revisions. I was urged to get rid of a character, bring another character into the spotlight, and change the ending. How should I change the ending? It was suggested that I should bring things together. Ah, of course, bring things together. I slashed one character, and brought another closer to the foreground, but that was just the first stage of the revising process. The ending needed a great deal of thought and much reworking. My editor didn't hold my hand through this (there were no pages sent back to me covered with pencil markings). It was just clear that work needed to be done. I began to ask myself questions about the entire revising process. I began, in fact, to be my own most ruthless editor.

With my first poetry book, *Light Falls Through You*, most things were easy to revise, but the novel was different. It was one of the hardest things I've ever done. It was also satisfying in a way that nothing else could be: I was creating a world and living both inside and outside it simultaneously. I was heartened when I got assistance from Joan Clark, who said that my novel manuscript simply needed to be finished. I was also encouraged by John Steffler, whose own first novel, *The Afterlife of George Cartwright*, had intrigued me. He observed that each new novelist has to invent a way to write the novel, no matter how many instructive books he or she has read on the subject. Until then, I laboured under the illusion that most other aspiring writers didn't flounder quite so much in the writing of a novel. Not so, he told me. Everyone flounders. Some get into trouble at the beginning, others discover that the middle of the novel sags, and a few throw up their hands as they're nearing the end.

I'd read quite a lot about writing fiction (when I teach fiction workshops, I often fall back on Janet Burroway's *Writing Fiction: A Guide to Narrative Craft*), but no book can possibly offer the *only* way through such a complex process. I had to find my own way through it, and I'm not the kind who can plan it out carefully in advance. I've now written two novels, and I didn't really know how things would end in either one when I began them. I thought, and still do, that such knowledge would make it into a paint-by-numbers picture. So I knew the main things that were going to happen, but I allowed for change if that was going to help the story along. On the other hand, I thought hard about what I wanted to get across in my first novel: a story that revealed how people act as individuals within the confines, and the freedom, of family. I wanted to examine how men talk to women, how women talk to men, how men talk to men, and how women talk to women.

I knew that somewhere along the line there would be a cost — probably a huge cost — to at least one of the characters, and that I would have to grit my teeth and write it. For me, the big story didn't have to be all about action. It had to be about character, and how people respond to things that happen to them, or how they make mistakes and have to live through them, or how they rub up against other people with startling consequences: good, bad, ugly.

There's much to be said for the idea that revising starts even before the novel is begun. I spend some time writing down ideas. I drink coffee and write notes, and pretend I'm doing something toward writing a novel, though there are times when I think I might as well be knitting. I write bits and pieces, and even parts of chapters, all of which help me see the novel more clearly, though later on I usually toss these fragments. They are simply attempts at thinking things through, but what I'm after is the book's core. Still, even if there's been a lot of thinking about the narrative beforehand, revision — to literally *re-vision* or see things again — is what I continue to do as I write my way into, and through, the book.

It's also what I do as I write my way out of the book. Two things need to be considered after the first, second, or third draft has been written: what needs to be added and what needs to be cut. I think in the case of any writer, it's harder to accomplish the latter than the former. But revision is meant to be radical. As William Faulkner said, "Kill your darlings." I don't know how many darlings I've killed, but there have been a lot, and it may not have been enough. They keep appearing, those darlings. Radical revising means that the writer is prepared to rework the story, novel, or essay, almost as if he or she was not the one who wrote it to begin with. Annie Dillard talks about revision as if the writer were building a house:

The line of words is a hammer. You hammer lightly against the walls of your house. You tap the walls, lightly, everywhere. After giving many years' attention to these things, you know what to listen for. Some of the walls are bearing walls; they have to stay, or everything will fall down. Other walls can go with impunity; you can hear the difference. Unfortunately, it is often a bearing wall that has to go. It cannot be helped. There is only one solution, which appalls you, but there it is. Knock it out. Duck.[1]

As soon as I read those words, I knew what Dillard meant. The best question that anyone ever asked me was this: Is it a good story? It's not enough to say, "Well, I've worked really hard on it." Always, for me, the issue of whether or not a novel is a good story is of prime importance. And to make my manuscript into a good story, I had to throw away much of what I'd done. So out went a bearing wall in my novel. I changed the point of view from first person singular to third person omniscient. Hundreds of pages were taken out, especially those that seemed to veer off from the main story. I dropped a character, because I was dealing with a family and there were too many people. The job of keeping them intact and somehow separate in my head — and staying on top of which one had a scar on his nose or which one had blue eyes — was almost more than I could manage.

It's different for every writer, but now I have a few questions I ask myself when I start to revise:

1. Does the beginning call the reader into the story?
2. Are the characters real people (that is, do they talk and interact the way real people do)?
3. What changes for the characters, and how do the characters change as a result?
4. Does the story have an ineluctable force that reveals things that must happen, and finally end in an almost inevitable, but not predictable, way?
5. Is it a good story?

I haven't mentioned plot among these questions. The reason for this is that I'm convinced that things happen to people because of the way they respond to, or anticipate, events in their lives. A character might be hit by a car because he's been running down a dirt road at night to get away from his girlfriend. Granted, some things just crop up, but more often they happen because a character responds erratically to something, or misjudges a situation. Something shifts, and a character rises to the situation, or falls under its weight. This, to me, is what transforms a situation into a string of actions, and actions into plot. The most significant issue is change, rather than plot. (What changes? Who changes? Why?) Yet all five questions help to determine whether or not the novel accumulates power as it goes along. In the end, I often can't answer these questions very well; I don't tick them off. I merely ask them, and in asking them, I think about them.

Virginia Woolf stresses the difficulties of writing fiction in *A Room of One's Own*, as she points out that "for the most part, novels come to grief somewhere. The imagination falters under the enormous strain. The insight is confused . . ."[2] There is a sense that novels come to light only after the most arduous of revisions. So how do writers know when they get it right? Here again, Woolf's comments are apt (she points out that the novel she has in mind is *War and Peace*), because it is clear that the integrity of the work is what counts:

> What one means by integrity, in the case of the novelist, is the conviction that he gives one that this is the truth. Yes, one feels, I should never have thought that this could be so; I have never known people behaving like that. But you have convinced me that so it is, so it happens.[3]

This benchmark is one of the best I know, because it pushes the writer to test herself against it. In my case, when I finished my initial revisions, I knew I wasn't finished. Did I have an ending that gave "the conviction . . . [of] the truth"? No, I didn't. Not yet. Somewhere along the line, I realized that while I was busy revising the first two-thirds of the novel, the last third had gone virtually unnoticed. A rigorous, but kind, mentor got me to pay attention to this, long before I spoke to the editor at Penguin Canada. Someone else said: "You can't put a beach in the title and not get the reader to the beach." Exactly. But I needed someone to say it to me, and not just once, but several times. What was I going to do with all the characters, crowding around, vying for attention? If I didn't focus the energy of the novel, it would have been like throwing a surprise party and not providing a cake.

I have a feeling now that the ending is the hardest part of a novel. Somehow it has to contain the wisdom of the whole book in a casual, subtle way, but it also has to be gripping, even if there aren't a lot of action-packed events. And I think of the last third of the novel as the most critical section. It was only after many revisions that it came to me that I had to go much deeper. I had to gather things together and allow a natural sliding away at the same time.

And, of course, even though I knew my characters had to learn something, I hadn't been allowing them to learn. But as I went deeper, I found that it was possible. After years of working on my novel, I finally saw how to make it into a story that was complete in itself. I didn't know if I could do it, but at least I had a glimpse of it. In the case of my revisions to *Canterbury Beach*, the moment of discovery came when I saw that one of the characters had to reveal something that would either have the effect of tearing his family apart or bringing it together. So I had to go backward, to a chapter in the book that preceded the last four or five, before I could go forward to the ending. I didn't have any idea of this beforehand. I thought I could simply rewrite the last four or five chapters. But no, I had to go even further back in the novel. Then the revision of the ending was much easier to do.

What is it like, that "Oh my God, that's it!" kind of feeling, when we read something and it's right, so exactly right that there's nothing to be changed, nothing to be added? At the end of *The Writing Life*, Annie Dillard writes a chapter about the stunt pilot Dave Rahm, who was not just any stunt pilot:

> Like any fine artist, he controlled the tension of the audience's longing. You desired, unwittingly, a certain kind of roll or climb, or a return to a certain portion of the air, and he fulfilled your hope slantingly, like a poet, or evaded it until you thought you would burst, and then fulfilled it surprisingly, so you gasped and cried out.[4]

I think this is what all writers are trying for, that looping and wheeling through the wild blue yonder up above the earth, when something has been abandoned down below. It's a rare feeling. It's true that when I'm doing revisions, I often prefer to be planting bulbs in the garden. I'd rather go on to the next book, out there on the alluring horizon. But when I'm truly immersed in revising, I sometimes find myself stunt flying. I finally see how the revising of a manuscript is the writing of it. I have a vision of the whole thing; I see what I've been trying to do all along. This is what we want more than anything else: a line of words that spin and roll, and spiral and knife through the air, and then land, softly, back on earth again.

1. Annie Dillard, *The Writing Life* (New York: Harper & Row, 1984), 4.
2. Virginia Woolf, *A Room of One's Own* (1928; reprint, Harmondsworth, England: Penguin Books, 1973), 73.
3. Woolf, 72.
4. Dillard, 96.

Jacklighting

PUBLISHING NON-FICTION is safe enough if the work stays within the fact-based boundaries of subjects like West Coast mixed stock fishery management, or other strictly defined topics. The writer who knows how to structure her work has only to plough the appropriate data wide and deep, consult enough knowledgeable people, and fact-check obsessively.

Similar rigorous efforts guarantee nothing, let alone safety, once creative non-fiction is published. A measure of danger is built into creative non-fiction, a.k.a. fooling around with the linear presentation of facts, as in *Voyages at Sea with Strangers,* a book about offshore fishery observer work on board Canadian trawlers, as well as Russian and Polish fishing ships. The book was made from experiences encoded in words, which had been scratched into Rite-in-the-Rain notebooks, while I was standing at the stern minding the haul. "Rybitwa = sea bird" and "coffee beans, grind" were set alongside fish estimates: " Tow #107 22 metric tons hake; 600 kilograms dogfish? 400 kilograms yellowtail. Check Loran." Late at night, images of salted rust patterns on the gear, or a porthole-framed ocean sometimes made their way onto draft pages of factory diagrams. These pages, shoved into back pockets, were always found weeks later, laundered into barely legible fragments.

When HarperCollins first released *Voyages*, I was at sea again. A means of escape might be the only advantage of writing creative non-fiction while living it.

After the fishing season, I discovered that although interviewers and critics cannot accuse the supposedly literary non-fiction writer of creating unbelievable characters or scenes, one reviewer had suggested I was likely crazy to live and record such a grim existence. More than ten years later, I still sorrow over that dismissive comment. It had occurred to me that I was crazy, but not that life at sea was grim.

Only the book interview for Newfoundland's Fisheries Broadcast was comfortable. On the tape, I can hear my ease with an interviewer undaunted by accounts of hard work and storms, as well as laughter. In Newfoundland, I didn't worry about looking like a preoccupied mouse photographed beside a red-hulled grain ship on the book's cover. Instead, I recalled entertaining my next Russian crew with the Toronto photographer's unfulfilled wish that I supply atmosphere by summoning the offshore fishing fleet into Vancouver's harbour. The Russians were all for running fifty hours in a November gale to prove they were good for atmosphere, but we had to haul the damn cod end knowing it would hold no hake that night.

Voyages received some good reviews, although bookstores were unsure of its place: Travel? Adventure? Memoir? Belles lettres? When *Moving Water*, a novel, was published a few years later, I was pit-lamped again. Jacklighting, it might be called in some parts of the country, meaning hunting in the dark with a fierce light to transfix the eyes of writers and other wild creatures. At readings, I noticed myself choosing the sections of *Moving Water* nearest to the safety of fact-based non-fiction.

Still, I might find out where to get those Rite-in-the-Rain notebooks, even if I'm not actually, factually, writing creative non-fiction in the rain any more.

Don't Do Anything but **Write**

OTTAWA. My first novel begins with a fascination that visits, settles in, and will not leave. I'm living on Bank Street in an apartment with one window, a ventilation shaft, and dead cockroaches on the grey carpet. I begin scratching down notes, something about a magician, an Egyptian myth of royalty, a brother and sister who lead lives of crime together after dark. I then stash the notes away in a drawer and forget about them for ten years.

Vancouver. A decade later, on the other side of the country. I'm surprised to discover that the story is still there, alive and pulsing. Demanding to be written. And so, I begin. Again. I do the Anvil Press 3-Day Novel Contest over Labour Day weekend. It's still warm outside, so I take my notebook down to the beach. I alternate lying on my stomach writing circus scenes with quick dips in the ocean. It's not so bad, this business of being a writer.

In the following three years that it takes me to see this novel through to completion, I will move five times. Three different provinces, three different cities, west to east. In her book, *Break Every Rule*, Carole Maso writes, "Home is the luminous imagination."[1] Like me, she has moved around a lot. When I find this sentence in her essay, "The Shelter of the

Alphabet," I jot it down on a piece of paper. To remind myself that wherever I am, writing is there with me.

Montreal. I have fallen in love. I'm living off my savings and writing full-time. The door is wide open. I collect everything, all characters, all scenes. I write down words, snippets, clues, without knowing what they are, or what they may become. One day I'm in the locker room at the gym without any paper, so I scratch a scene down on the inside of a ripped-open box of Vick's lemon cough drops. I say yes to what presents itself, knowing that the winnowing will happen later.

On winter days, I go to the neighbourhood café and write in my notebook. Through my headphones, I listen to Beethoven and Mozart. Music without voices, so I can hear what's going on in my head. I write scenes, images, fragments.

Some days I stay in the apartment, while outside the window near my desk snow falls thick and soft. I drink hot chocolate. I type the handwritten scenes into the computer. In this way, I'm writing a book.

I read *Writing*, a book of essays by Marguerite Duras, one of the last books she wrote before her death in 1996. Her work has mentored me since I discovered it in university. It has taught me the value of silence, of leaving spaces in the language where readers can enter, pause, breathe, move around. It has taught me the value of contradiction. The beauty of a text where different possibilities can exist together in the same lines. The value of ambiguity between the white of the paper and the black of the words.

Raymond Queneau told Marguerite Duras: "Don't do anything but write."[2] I find this sentence and copy it into my notebook.

Some days, there is only a single image, a shard. Some days, nothing. Other days, pages appear. It's surprising how much courage is required to float words through the void.

I take a workshop through the Quebec Writers' Federation and receive feedback on portions of the manuscript. Gradually, the scenes and fragments begin to assume the ghost of a shape, but it's slippery and keeps morphing into something new. I develop extrasensory perception and keep an eye on the ghost until it begins to solidify. Then I ask it to please hold still before pinning it to the ground and tracing its outline with a black, waterproof pen.

During one phase of the writing, there's a ritual. Always in the morning, not too early. Steaming tea in a favourite cup, muffin and fruit on a green plate. The sun making its way across the room, against the back of my head. I draw the curtain. There's the satisfying tap-tap of my fingers against the plastic of the keyboard as I transfer handwritten sections onto disk.

Marguerite Duras: "One can go who knows where, no doubt toward the adoration of the sister, the love story between sister and brother, still, yes, for all eternity, a dazzling, inconsiderate, punished love."[3] She was talking about one of her own books of course, not mine. It was pure coincidence that I was telling the story of a brother and sister, a pair of dazzling twins blessed with eternal love and delicate self-punishments.

Banff. I get to spend five weeks at the Centre for the Arts. I am to do nothing but work on the novel, to live and breathe writing. I learn so much here. I find a community of other writers, artists, musicians. I get editorial feedback on my manuscript from published authors. I have an ID card that says ARTIST. I eat many good desserts, and begin to feel less like a fake.

Toronto. I end up in this city without planning to. I continue to write. There is help along the way. The Canada Council phones to confirm my mailing address. My horoscope in the *Toronto Star* reads: "A dream has come true, but you may not know it yet." A few weeks later, I find out I've been awarded the grant I applied for. I am jubilant and weed out all distractions. I focus my energy. I put everything I've got into the novel.

There are:

Times when there is no writing.
Trips to the art gallery.
Long walks.
Entire days spent in bed, sleeping and dreaming.
Tears, doubts.
Uncountable hours of reading.
And always, the faithful returns to writing.

Marguerite Duras: "A writer is often quite restful; she listens a lot."[4] I'm at my desk doing some more research on my main character's condition: conscious starvation. I'm wearing a shirt with dragons on it and thinking of the way a story gets shaped from a parade of words. I'm thinking of the ability of language to shine.

Different people read sections and versions of the manuscript at points along the way. I take all comments under consideration. I sift through, keeping what fits. I revise. I write more. I revise. I write more. The book grows.

I become impossible to live with. Everyone walks too slowly. All sounds are too loud. Nothing is neat enough. All smells are too strong. I have to sleep alone. I can't sleep. A friend says it's like my nerves are extending five feet outside my body. I exhibit signs of pregnancy. A bloated belly. Swollen breasts. Of course, of course. I'm pregnant with this book. Meanwhile, people around me are having babies and I can't hold them. All I can hold is this book. Sometimes it feels perverse to be so full of something that isn't human.

I finish a "final" draft. I give it to some writer friends to read and am immediately assailed by an unexpected emptiness. Unanchored without the manuscript, I am capable only of sitting on the couch, watching television, collapsing into vacancy. I begin to develop an understanding of the phrase, hurry up and wait.

During this time, the second novel begins to reveal itself to me. One day, I'm walking down the street and the idea materializes from out of nowhere. I can see now how it had been invisibly building itself in the back of my imagination, like iron filings moving toward a magnet, while I lived my life in the outside world, oblivious.

I start a file folder for the new book. A place to collect the details that are beginning to coalesce into living bodies, the scenes that are playing themselves out in a parallel world. I write things down on scraps of paper and slip them in there, while the book quietly forms crystals beneath my skin.

Finally, I get the last round of feedback. I revise the manuscript again. I fine-tune, change words and phrases, fill in gaps, add missing connective tissue. I begin to get a sense of completion, and there's an excitement building somewhere behind my ribs. The thrill of becoming real.

The final draft is accepted by Coach House Books in October. My book will come out in the spring. There are things to do.

And there are " The Worries":

That people will think the book is about me, my life.
That it will offend somebody, everybody.
That it is too simplistic.
That it is too complicated.
That the language is too poetic.

That it is too prosaic.

That it hasn't taken me a lifetime to write.

That it has taken me far too long to get to this place.

Then there is editing. The seemingly endless tinkering. I add tiny missing details, check for consistency, look for the perfect word. I have to decide what is pure indulgence and must be axed. There is painstaking poring over sentences, and reading them aloud to see how they vibrate together. It's hard work, but when it's through, I have a manuscript that is much more like I imagined it could be. This is a good thing.

Next there are decisions about cover design, author photo, book size. I decide on 8"x 5" because it's the same size as the copy of Duras's *The War* I happen to be carrying in my shoulder bag. I see the first copy printed and bound on the press. It's exciting and strange. A small, green book exists in the world that wasn't there before, and I've written it. My life looks the same on the outside, but feels different on the inside. I was warned of this.

I give readings in Toronto, Ottawa, Vancouver. There are a handful of reviews, good and bad. Some people laud the book's language, while others find it irritating. I try not to let any of it get to me. People will have their opinions, I tell myself. Though I notice it's the critical comments that lodge in my mind. Sneaky thorns.

Now, fourteen years after making those first notes that became *How the Blessed Live*, I'm back in Ottawa, scribbling away on a short story collection. I can barely stand to listen to Mozart any more and I never thought I'd live in this city again. Life is a crackerjack box of surprises. I'm starting to get that it doesn't really matter where you are. What matters is what you're doing. And what I'm doing is writing.

1. Carole Maso, *Break Every Rule* (Washington, DC: Counterpoint, 2000), 18.

2. Marguerite Duras, *Writing* (Cambridge, MA: Lumen Editions, 1993), 3.

3. Duras, 20.

4. Duras, 13.

FRED STENSON

Lonesome
Hero

THE PUBLICATION of my first book, *Lonesome Hero*, was so long ago, thirty years, that remembering the details is a challenge. The year was 1974. The publisher was Macmillan of Canada. The means was the Search-For-An-Alberta-Novelist Competition of 1972, in which I was a finalist alongside Cecelia Frey (*Breakaway*), and behind the winner Jan Truss (*Bird at the Window*). I had written the book in a mad hurry during the first three months of a long-saved-for year of backpacking through Europe, and the typing and submitting of the manuscript became a family and community project after I sent several scribblers full of scribble and a begging letter home to Twin Butte, Alberta.

The news that my novel was going to be published came to me by phone in the cavernous backroom of a German bakery, where I was scrubbing cake pans and cookie sheets with a big brush. I was the happiest young man alive. For all my efforts to write the book and have it considered in the competition, it seldom occurred to me that anything would come of it. It was one of those rare times in life when the brain is manoeuvring its parts at high speed, like a pachinko game. My prospects in the world; my imagined life story; my immediate future; my sense of myself — all were in flux.

I came home. I went to work on the farm for the winter, feeding cows. I received my novel from Toronto in sections full of suggested revisions, which I carried out with great seriousness on the Arborite table in the kitchen with the light on its adjustable cord pulled low. I fantasized about what great things might be happening to me if I were elsewhere.

By early spring, I had extricated myself from the farm — I'm not too proud of that part — and I went to Edmonton to live, believing for some reason that I would enter a kind of salon life and meet many brainy and beautiful women who wanted to be writers too.

What I did enter was the legion of the poor, living in a wartime, jerry-built, three-storey slum: bathroom a very long walk down a corridor neither level nor lit; neighbours who were some of them packed into their rooms like cord wood, and others living alone with odd habits — necromancy, terrible but loud singing, numerology.

While I waited for my first book to be published (such a long wait), I worked in a shipping-receiving warehouse, unloading boxcars full of baler twine. Once, I snuck aboard the forklift (how hard could it be?) and triggered a domino effect among towering columns of pallets. That I wasn't immediately fired taught me that Canada is an almost too forgiving place. At night, I wrote a second novel, about a tense standoff between a father and son on a southern Alberta ranch. My motives weren't pure. It wasn't going well.

While I was failing to write this novel, on days when I wasn't unloading baler twine, I would hang out at the HUB complex at the University of Alberta, looking for brainy, beautiful women to tell about my upcoming book. The person I did meet was Bart, an overweight entomologist who was failing to write his Ph.D. thesis. We met over a mutual fondness for one of those old pinball machines that is full of quirks and tricks that, if learned, reward you with nearly free amusement for hours. Bart would tell me about his strange advisor who would not approve his science-altering thesis proposal. I would tell him about the turgid standoff in my novel. Then we'd play more pinball, or snooker, or drink beer. That we had very little money between us kept everything within reason.

Bart, too, was looking for brainy and beautiful women, but his size caused any group of women to immediately part like the Red Sea. We both believed that being a soon-to-be-published author would help in finding a girlfriend, if anybody actually knew about it. We debated the creation of a sign I could wear.

A very exciting occasion during the wait for the novel was when the grand old man of publishing, Hugh Kane, came to Edmonton and invited me up to his Hotel Macdonald room for a drink. He had the dust jacket for my novel and wanted to show it to me.

Hugh had an engaging and polite manner. He asked what I drank, and I lied and told him Scotch, without any ice. Small talk out of the way, he showed me the cover. It was a disaster. The jacket was of a grey material: what might happen if you made paper out of dryer lint. The cover picture was of a dark-haired young man — a bit like a young George Bush Jr., come to think of it, in the way that his eyes were too close to his nose to make biological sense. He looked troubled — well, actually, insane, as if he were contemplating an act of mass violence.

I looked and looked, feigning a calm and objective interest. I suspect there wasn't enough blood in my face to bleed if scratched. Hugh said, "Ugly, isn't it?"

"Why," I asked, smiling as if the irony of a homely cover amused me, "why is it so ugly?"

And Hugh Kane, in his good storytelling style, explained the life fact that designers won't read the books they design for, so it is necessary to explain the book to them. He said he had a soft spot for *Lonesome Hero*, and so had gone to considerable lengths to explain its young hero: the mixture of humour and angst, and '70s pop culture. The cover image that came back was a big, lantern-jawed, John-Wayne type. He rejected it, explained again, got the new one — and they were out of time.

I asked for another Scotch.

Later in the session, I asked him how long he thought it would take me to be self-sufficient as a novelist. He said ten years. Ten years?! Little did I realize that he was probably understating the time deliberately by a decade; or maybe he believed it would never come to pass.

When *Lonesome Hero* finally saw the light of day, with its bad cover and all its parts, it was November 4, 1974. Jan Truss, Cecelia Frey, and I went on a little publicity tour. I think it was entirely inside Edmonton. I was greatly excited to be on radio and television; to see my face and name in the newspaper. I got a good review from Kildare Dobbs in *The Globe and Mail* and achieved levitation for a week or so.

And I did, on occasion, meet a brainy and beautiful young woman who wanted to write. On the most conspicuous of these occasions, the girl's father (a writer!) intervened and spirited her away and back on the track of her promising future. That too was an important life lesson.

VALERIE WEISS

Coming Clean

The Surfacing of a First Film

I STAND BESIDE the Dead Sea, covering myself with its mystical mud.

This is the prelude to a dream I had shortly after finishing my first film — a one-hour experimental documentary called *Timepiece*. It took me five years to complete and almost drove me insane. Passion, frustration, and a sense of purpose fuelled me, compelled me. But I'm not the same person I was when that first fusion of ideas surfaced and took over my life. The expectations I had in the beginning turned on me. Yet one thing is very clear: I was meant to make this film. That conviction has not deviated since day one. Giving myself the permission to do it began a series of questions, which rippled out and permeated every aspect of my life. And things haven't been the same since. Thank God.

I was tired of always talking about "someday" making my own film. I was tired of using the term "someday" in all of the areas of my life. I got angry — no, furious — and decided enough! I took that anger, that energy, and channelled it. I got working.

When you decide to delve into the murky waters of your past and bring it to the surface, its force resonates through every cell of your being. Making a film about how my family survived the Holocaust, and its subsequent

135

effect on *my* life, compelled me to deal with a lot of personal issues. I found myself face to face with things that had long ago buried themselves so deep that no one knew they existed.

Because I was the youngest of five children, maybe my mother had more time to tell me stories of how she survived the Holocaust. In 1979, she decided it was time to go back to Hungary. This was her first trip back since the war. It was also my father's first time back since leaving at the age of nine. I was the only child to go with my parents on that trip.

Hearing the stories while actually walking through the streets, seeing the building where my mother and grandmother hid during the war, feeling those intense feelings as memory after memory surged up and re-enacted itself for my mother was possibly more than I, at the age of fourteen, could deal with at the time. I remember seeing her weep when we visited the "summer house," the epitome of her innocent childhood before the war, as it lay crumbled and neglected before us. That trip hit me hard. Only I didn't know it at the time. It lay submerged, dormant — only to surface twenty years later as I made the film.

Growing up as I did in safe, quiet, suburban Don Mills, Ontario, the terror of war, bombs, and torture and death for being Jewish seemed inconceivable. A bad dream. I grew up in a household that simply wanted to move on, blend in. I knew nothing about Judaism. It was simply this vague term for something I was — but little else. It had no connection with my day-to-day life. For my father, who came from an Orthodox family, it only seemed to ignite fury. What value did religion have when his Orthodox father would vanish to pray, while his mother was left to care for ten kids? What value did Judaism have when his father eventually abandoned the family, leaving his mother to care for them on her own in Canada during the Depression? For my mother, religion represented something that only divided people and caused wars. It wasn't high on the priority list.

As I delved into my family's past, issues of identity were brought to the forefront. The terror I felt every step of the way while making the film seemed inextricably linked to how I saw and expressed myself, my ideas, my life. Diving in with no sense of what lurked in the waters below proved to be a formidable challenge.

For my mother, there's always been this sense that disaster lurks at every turn. Considering what she went through during the war, this outlook on life made sense. I came to realize that I also had this view of life. But, until I began working on the film, I didn't understand why. I couldn't connect this way of dealing with things in my life to any concrete event or experience. I started to realize that this attitude affected how I functioned in the world. One of the film's themes is how my mother and grandparents' experience continues to influence me; that the impact of one's history can resonate long after the actual events have occurred. I became interested in learning more about Judaism, exploring it as a culture and a religion. The process of learning more about my culture has been about discovering who I am, swimming through the elemental waters of my being, and finding something deeper in life on both a spiritual and religious level. I've been learning how to be comfortable in my own skin and not hide anymore.

But all of this only came later. When I began working on the film, I had a whole range of goals and expectations. I wanted to document my family's history to preserve it for future generations, to do something with real meaning and finally fulfill the dream of making my own film. I wanted to show the world that I had something valuable to say. I also wanted to use it to further my editing career. If I happened to move into a producing or directing career, all the better.

When I first started talking about making a film, I don't think anyone in my family really believed me. But, as I began shooting, the reality started to sink in. They were all curious. My parents, especially my mother, couldn't fathom what I was up to. I decided not to show my family anything until the film was close to being finished. It was a protective device I believed would help me to remain objective, clear, and focused on making the movie I intended.

Often I found myself running away, wanting to escape from my family. The film was so personal and intense that I needed space. This was very difficult for them to understand. As the months dragged into years, it was a real test of patience — for them and for me. My mother and I are exceptionally close. At times, too close. I was using the film to come to terms with our relationship, to put our unique bond in perspective. There were many times when I would be frustrated or tense, but unable to discuss my feelings with her. Most of the film's narration is my mother telling her story; I was hearing her voice every day in the edit suite. Often, after a day of working on the film, the last thing I wanted to do was see or talk to her. I know this was incredibly hard on her. I think she felt guilty; worried that other people might think she had put me up to this. I kept reminding her that this was something I wanted and needed to do.

Several times I asked myself, " Why did I have to take on something so personal, so heavy, for my first film? Why didn't I begin with a nice little two-minute short film instead?" Feeling crazy, ostracized, and lonely, I would look around and feel as though everyone around me was doing much more logical (or socially acceptable) things with their time and money. I seriously questioned my sanity many times. The potent combination of handling one's family history, especially such a profound experience, along with being a total perfectionist made the work especially difficult. Every move, every decision, felt immense. I wanted to do justice to my family's history. Can you think of anything more daunting?

I was my own worst enemy in terms of the pressure I placed on myself, constantly searching for the "right" way to do things. I also think I was looking for external approval. I remember, as the years went by, everyone constantly asking me, "So, when's the film gonna be done?" and feeling totally frustrated because they had *no idea* what was involved: the time, the money, the incredible emotional energy it consumed. Maybe I was doing it all wrong. By choosing not to show them anything concrete until it was closer to being finished, the concept of the film remained elusive. Added to this were several major conflicts with a crew member. But somehow these moments of incredible doubt, fear, and simply not knowing what to do always gave way to ... you've *got* to do this. Making the film gave me a sense of purpose. My creative juices had been restrained for so long watching others make films. This liberated them. I went from watching others "do" to becoming a "doer" myself.

I actually never thought I'd be "allowed" to finish the film, fearing that ultimately something or someone would get in the way of its being shown; that my dream of making a film would be left unfulfilled. I had to dig deep and keep reassuring myself that I could do this — that I *needed* to do this. I think that some of my fears were similar to my mother's — that disaster lurks at every turn. I would have these dreams of arriving to show the film at a theatre, only to find out that the film had been destroyed by someone who was angry with me, or that the film projector didn't work properly. In another dream, I arrived at the theatre, full of people waiting to view it, only to realize that the film didn't exist!

Once a satisfactory edit of the film was complete, I invited my parents for a private screening of my opus. I was terrified. What if they didn't like it? What if my mother demanded changes? I still shake thinking about it. But, as the closing music ended, all my mother and I could do was cry. My father was stunned. The film really did exist.

Shortly thereafter, my mother went into a panic. She called, asking me where I intended to show the film and what type of groups would be viewing it. I was bewildered by the question. After much discussion, I got to the core of her fears. Fifty years after the war, she told me that she was still worried about people finding out that we are Jewish, about an anti-Semitic group coming after us and killing us. I was stunned. I tried to calm her down as best I could. I argued with her that I hadn't made this film only to see it locked away, that it was about sharing our story and showing who we are to the world. It was about accepting the risks involved in revealing our story. There was no turning back.

Once I finished the film, the roller-coaster ride continued. There have been the high points: the exhilaration (and terror) of showing the film publicly for the first time, the excitement of getting positive reviews and being interviewed on TV. There have been the amazing discussions that have come up after showing the film. I've seen it touch others and make them think. I've felt the immense satisfaction of completing something so personally important, knowing I'm happy with the finished product and that I *did it!*

There have also been the low points: the strange feeling of emptiness once the film's premiere was over; the "Now what?" feelings; the negative reviews; applying to many film festivals and not getting selected; feeling the pressure of the questions, "So, are you going to make another film? What's it going to be about?" and having no answer.

Something changed during the years it took me to make *Timepiece*. Several times I've told people that I think the process "spoiled" me. Maybe it was so satisfying doing something truly creative that to go back to working on another shlocky television series or formulaic feature film, if only to make a living, was no longer enough. Maybe all of those years spent honing my skills in film were really meant for making *Timepiece*. All I know is that something shifted inside me. I decided that I needed to put my energy toward something more valuable and directly beneficial to others. After much soul-searching, I decided to leave the world of film.

I sometimes stop, look around, and am shocked at how different my life is now. I am surrounded by so many amazing people, live with a wonderful partner, and now have a beautiful son. My mother and I are still very close, but now I feel like my life is my own; that we are separate people with different lives. The person who began making the film is dead; someone else has been formed and has risen to the surface. Ultimately, making the film was an act of purification; it's like I've come clean.

The
String
Box

IT WAS THE MID-1960s. I was writing short pieces for an afternoon program on CBC radio. Some of my stories were fantasy, some were about events of the day, some were historical. I used to go to the old CBC building on Jarvis Street in Toronto to record them. My talks, I was told, were a leavening event in the more serious parts of the hour. In other words, I was the comic relief. I'd been doing it for some time when one day, the producer said, "Your pieces are getting kind of weird, Rachel, maybe you need to write a novel." As I was leaving his office, he called out, "And make it picaresque!"

I was about thirty-six then and I'd always thought I'd like to have a novel published before I was forty, so it seemed like a good idea. I went home and looked up "picaresque" in the dictionary and began to write. The Smith Corona portable typewriter I'd used for years was about to earn its keep.

———

HOW DID I MANAGE to write a novel with four children, three of whom were attending a school I could see from the garden and who came home for lunch? My neighbour across the road said she could set her clocks by the time she saw my head appear in the window above my desk. I had about two hours free until it was time to get out the bread and peanut butter and jelly. I wrote and I wrote and I wrote. I figured I was putting everything I'd ever known, thought, felt, been, seen, and enjoyed into those twenty chapters. This was it. I would never write another book. There would be nothing left to write. And every page was typed onto a carbon paper sandwich. Nice white paper on top, onion skin beneath. I did a great deal of retyping and used a litre or so of whiteout per chapter.

—

FINALLY, there it was. A pile of paper. A picaresque novel. Not a fraction of the length of *Don Quixote* but mine own. I called it *The String Box*. To understand why, read the book. So what next? Who would want it? I didn't hand it around to friends and relatives to read in case they told me it was boring, or worse, imagined the characters to be based on them and sued. I found a book in the library about publishers and decided to begin with the best. Off the package went to McClelland and Stewart in Toronto, and after a week, I began to look for the letter of acceptance.

We were moving at the time from Oakville to an old farmhouse in the Niagara Peninsula. We had trouble getting the mail at first. There was a line of those rural boxes down at the end of the lane. The previous owners had taken their box with them and we put in a new one. Days went by and no mail arrived. At last we went to the post office in the village to ask why. It was easy, our box was not the right height for the mailman to lean out of the window of his van and put the letters into. Well then, could they just give us our mail as we were in the office, and we would go home and make sure our box was raised to the same level as the others — a matter of about nine inches? No, they couldn't. It had to be delivered. We pulled up the post and adjusted the height, and we got mail.

Eventually, a nice letter came from Jack McClelland. It had good points, my novel, and they'd be interested in whatever else I did, but *The String Box* was not for them.

I then sent it to a smaller publisher of good repute. Again with the waiting. Not that I was idly sitting down the lane by the mailbox. With four children and a menagerie of assorted animals, my time wasn't entirely my own. After six months, I inquired of the publisher what had become of my manuscript. Nothing. He was sorry to say that it appeared to be lost. It had arrived at the office, but was now nowhere to be found. Profound regrets, etc. That fellow went out of business soon after. Nothing to do with me.

Dismayed but not destroyed, I began to read the book reviews in newspapers more carefully and found a piece about a new book that sounded similar to mine, in the sense of being a bit offbeat. All I had left was the onion skin copy. With what I see now as foolhardiness, I sent that off to the publisher named in the review. Ten days later, I received a letter from Dennis Lee. The House of Anansi Press would be pleased to publish *The String Box*.

I was overwhelmed and just the easy side of forty.

I was too overwhelmed to look carefully at the contract, but I'm sure it was fair.

There followed a couple of editing sessions at the farmhouse kitchen table with Dennis. I mainly remember a great deal of laughter. Two of his admonitions have remained in my mind: Don't editorialize. And, please, don't write the next one on toilet paper.

The proofs came. Proofs! The importance of the word sent me out to stare at the frogs in the pond for a while. I had proofs! My children helped me by reading aloud from the manuscript, while I carefully went over the proofs to clear up the mistakes.

The wrong set of proofs went to the printer, and so there's a handful of typos in every chapter. That was only the beginning of the adventures of *The String Box*. Publication day. The arrival of the books. A delightful cover. In spite of the errors, it was well-reviewed in *The Globe and Mail* and elsewhere, and I began to feel like a writer and waited for the fame and the fortune to be delivered to the door.

I can't remember if I received an advance or any royalties, but I expect I did. Whatever the amount, it didn't, as they say, change my life. Some time later, there was a disastrous fire at the place where the Anansi books were stored. Water damage did in a lot of them, *The String Box* too. (I do have a few copies, of great value should there be a demand.)

I was asked to give a reading from the book, and this too was an amazing event for me. I prepared with care, choosing a section I thought would amuse, practising, timing myself. The four readers that evening were all first novelists and I was last on the list, my name being what it is. The woman before me read on and on and on and on. She looked up, finally, and said she'd just had to keep going because her book was so interesting. The audience was dead. I had misgivings about readings after that for a while. But the egoists who go on too long are few, and any writer who has been to the writing program at Banff during my tenure knows that reading over the allotted time is a sin right up there with Envy, Pride, Anger, and the rest.

And then there was the call from the movie director. My novel had been recommended to him. We met for lunch in Toronto. I was excited. The whole family was excited. We spent time over the dinner table choosing stars for the various roles. I would of course write the script. He just needed to raise three million dollars and we'd be in business. He would call me. That was 1972. I haven't heard back yet.

The String Box was never reprinted, never won a prize. Hundreds of copies ended up a soggy mass of pulp. But like old soldiers, books don't die. It's right there, at the top of my PLR list every year, hanging around in libraries across the country, perhaps being borrowed every now and then. And even read.

Biographies

Kelley Aitken

Kelley Aitken's *Love in a Warm Climate* (1998) was nominated for the Commonwealth Prize, Best First Book, Canadian Caribbean Region. Kelley is an artist, teacher, and illustrator. She lives with her partner in Toronto, Ontario.

Paul Anderson

Paul Anderson left Canada in his early twenties and spent much of the next fifteen years overseas. For the moment, he lives in Calgary, Alberta. *Hunger's Brides,* his first novel, was published by Random House Canada in September 2004.

Antonia Banyard

Antonia Banyard published *Seven Sisters* and *Lady Driven* with the Seven Sisters Writing Group (7swg.com). Her work has been published by literary magazines in Canada, Australia, England, and the United States. She attended The Banff Centre's writing studio in 1999 and completed a master's degree in writing from the University of Queensland in 2004.

bill bissett

first book eithr *we sleep inside each othr all or fires in th tempul* OR *th jinx ship n othr trips* 1965–66 2004 from talonbooks narrativ enigma / rumours uv hurricane 2003 cd rumours uv hurricane from red deer press as vizual artist shows at th pteros galleree toronto ontario poetree reedings canada u.s. europe n u.k

Paulette Dubé

Talon made the shortlists for the 1999 Canadian Literary Awards, the Alberta Writers' Guild Best Novel Award (2003), and the Starburst Award (2003). Best of all, Timothy Findley wrote a blurb for the back of the book!

From Jasper, Alberta, Paulette continues to write and teach, to fall and fly.

Eric Folsom

Eric Folsom is the author of *Poems for Little Cataraqui*, published by Broken Jaw Press, and subsequently, *What Kind of Love Did You Have In Mind?* and *Icon Driven*, both published by Wolsak and Wynn. He is writing a fourth book, a long poem about Nova Scotian history, while continuing to work at the Kingston Frontenac Public Library in Kingston, Ontario.

Sue Goyette

Sue Goyette's first book, *The True Names of Birds,* was published in 1998 by Brick Books. It's now in its sixth printing. She has also published a novel, *Lures* (HarperCollins, 2002), and another collection of poetry, *Undone* (Brick Books, 2004). Sue still lives in Nova Scotia and still wears black.

Elizabeth Greene

Elizabeth Greene is the editor of *We Who Can Fly*, a tribute to Adele Wiseman. She published the chapbook *The Moon Card* in 2001. She has published poems in the *Queen's Feminist Review* and appeared as Ms. January in the Ban Righ Centre 2005 calendar (if ever there was a place she didn't expect to end up).

Irene Guilford

Irene Guilford's novel *The Embrace* was published by Guernica Editions in 1999 and in Lithuanian translation by MacKaus Fondas (Chicago, 2002) and Baltos Lankos (Vilnius, 2003). She edited *Alistair MacLeod: Essays on His Works* (Guernica, 2001). She is at work on a second novel and various essays. She lives in Toronto, Ontario, with her husband.

Greg Hollingshead

Since *Famous Players* (1982), Greg Hollingshead has published two more story collections — *White Buick* (1992) and *The Roaring Girl* (1995) — and three novels: *Spin Dry* (1992), *The Healer* (1998), and *Bedlam* (2004). He lives in Edmonton, Alberta, where he has just retired from the University of Alberta. He is the director of the writing programs at The Banff Centre.

Helen Humphreys

Helen Humphreys' first book was a poetry collection, *Gods and Other Mortals*, published in 1986 by Brick Books. Since then she has written three other books of poetry and four novels, the most recent being *Wild Dogs*, published by HarperCollins in 2004. She lives in Kingston, Ontario.

Chris Koentges

The handsome twin-volume set that makes up *Towards An Erratic State* was published by Fox Run Press in the spring of 2004. Chris Koentges is currently finishing a book called

Homage To Any City for The Banff Centre Press. His National Magazine Award winning journalism has appeared in *The Walrus* and *The Globe and Mail* and on the CBC radio program *IDEAS*. His play, *Games For Midnight*, was produced by Ground Zero Theatre.

Jeanette Lynes

Jeanette Lynes is now the author of three books of poetry. Her most recent, *Left Fields* (Wolsak and Wynn), was a finalist for the 2003 Pat Lowther Memorial Award. She is the Poet Laureate for the Nova Scotia New Democratic Party and co-editor of *The Antigonish Review*.

Annabel Lyon

Annabel Lyon is a Vancouver fiction writer, freelancer, and teacher. Her first book, a collection of short stories entitled *Oxygen*, was published by Porcupine's Quill in 2000, and subsequently reprinted by McClelland and Stewart. Her second book, a trio of novellas entitled *The Best Thing for You*, was published in 2004. She is a regular contributor to *The Vancouver Sun*, *The Globe and Mail*, and *Geist* magazine.

Rick Maddocks

Rick Maddocks wrote *Sputnik Diner*. His non-fiction has since appeared in anthologies like *AWOL: True Tales for Travel-Inspired Minds* (Vintage, 2003), while a translation of his fiction appeared in *Vancouver: Roman d'une Ville* (Éditions Autrement: Paris, 2004). He teaches creative writing at Douglas College and performs music with the beige.

Don McKay

Since his first book, *Le Pendu*, things have improved for Don McKay. He has published seven books of poetry, including *Night Field*, for which he won the Governor General's Literary Award. He has served as editor and publisher of Brick Books since 1975, and is currently the senior poetry editor for The Banff Centre.

K. D. Miller

Since publishing *A Litany In Time of Plague*, K. D. Miller has produced a second collection of short stories, *Give Me Your Answer*, as well as *Holy Writ*, a collection of personal essays that explore the relationship between creativity and spirituality. She is currently at work on a novel, *October*. She lives in Toronto, Ontario.

Lorie Miseck

Lorie Miseck lives in Edmonton, Alberta. *A Promise of Salt* won the Wilfred Eggleston Award for non-fiction and was a finalist for the Writers' Trust of Canada Pearson's Prize and the City of Edmonton Book Prize. Her poetry collection is called *the blue not seen*.

Kim Moritsugu

Kim Moritsugu's first novel, *Looks Perfect*, was shortlisted for the Toronto

Book Award. She is also the author of a domestic comedy called *Old Flames*, and *The Glenwood Treasure,* a literary mystery that was a finalist for the Arthur Ellis Best Crime Novel Award.

Leilah Nadir

Leilah Nadir is an Iraqi-Canadian writer living in Vancouver, British Columbia. She is the author of a play, *Heavenly Bodies*, a collection of short stories, *Bazaar,* and a novel, *Still*. Since the invasion of Iraq, she has been writing and broadcasting political commentaries on CBC, in *The Globe and Mail,* and in the *Georgia Straight*, among others. She is currently working on a memoir about life in Iraq since the invasion, *The Sea of Gold*, and a novel, *The Orange Trees.*

Peter Oliva

Since the publication of *Drowning in Darkness*, Peter Oliva has published a second novel called *The City of Yes*. This book won the Writers' Trust of Canada Award and a FG Bressani Prize in 2000. He received a Canadian Bookseller's Association Award in 1999. The French translation of *Drowning in Darkness* was published by Gallimard in 2005.

Ruth Roach Pierson

Author of *"They're Still Women After All": The Second World War and Canadian Womanhood* (McClelland & Stewart, 1986), as well as other works of academic history, Ruth Roach

Pierson published her first book of poems, *Where No Window Was,* with BuschekBooks in 2002 and is currently at work on her second poetry manuscript, tentatively entitled "Burlap Coat."

Sina Queyras

Sina Queyras's first book of poetry, *Slip*, came out in 2001. Her second collection, *Teeth Marks*, was published in the fall of 2004. She recently edited an anthology of contemporary Canadian poetry for Persea Books of New York. Sina teaches creative writing at Rutgers University, and lives in Brooklyn, New York.

Gloria Sawai

Gloria Sawai's collection of short stories, *A Song for Nettie Johnson*, was published in 2001. In 2002, it received the Governor General's Literary Award for Fiction in English. Since its publication, Gloria has been working on a long story set on a rugged island off the coast of Norway.

Barbara Scott

Barbara Scott's first book, a collection of stories entitled *The Quick,* won the City of Calgary Book Prize, and the Writers Guild of Alberta Prize for short fiction. She is now poking around her second book, a novel, kicking up the dust, and smiling much of the time.

Anne Simpson

Anne Simpson's most recent poetry collection, *Loop* (2003), won the Griffin Poetry Prize and was a finalist for the Governor General's Literary Award. She has written a novel, *Canterbury Beach* (2001), and a previous book of poetry, *Light Falls Through You* (2000). She lives with her family in northeastern Nova Scotia.

Joan Skogan

Joan Skogan's first book, *Skeena: A River Remembered* (1983), was followed by three children's books; the memoir, *Voyages at Sea with Strangers* (1992); a novel, *Moving Water* (1998); and the recent non-fiction work, *Mary of Canada: The Virgin Mary in Canadian Culture, Spirituality, History, and Geography* (2003).

Susannah M. Smith

Susannah M. Smith's first novel, *How the Blessed Live*, was published by Coach House Books in 2002. She recently finished a second novel, *The Dummy Notebooks*, and is currently living in Ottawa, Ontario, where she is writing a short story collection.

Fred Stenson

After *Lonesome Hero* in 1974, Fred Stenson did not publish a novel again until *Last One Home* in 1988. In 2000, his novel *The Trade* was nominated for the Giller Prize. His most recent novel is *Lightning* (2004). He is the director of the Wired Writing Studio at The Banff Centre.

Valerie Weiss

Since completing *Timepiece*, Valerie has worked for a variety of arts and cultural organizations. Currently, she is doing consulting work after the recent birth of her son, Aaron. She may or may not make another film, but will continue to express herself in whatever creative medium her heart desires.

Rachel Wyatt

Before *The String Box,* Rachel wrote short pieces for newspapers, magazines, and radio. After that, she decided she was a novelist. The dreaded second novel didn't work out and became a radio play. The producer said, "We'll give you seven-fifty for this." Unused to large fees, she imagined a decimal point after the seven. She's now writing her sixth novel. Rachel still loves writing for the stage and being with actors, and is working on another play.